CLERGY
SEXUAL ABUSE
LITIGATION

CLERGY
SEXUAL ABUSE
LITIGATION

Survivors Seeking Justice

Jennifer M. Balboni

FIRST**FORUM**PRESS

A DIVISION OF LYNNE RIENNER PUBLISHERS, INC. • BOULDER & LONDON

Published in the United States of America in 2011 by
FirstForumPress
A division of Lynne Rienner Publishers, Inc.
1800 30th Street, Boulder, Colorado 80301
www.firstforumpress.com

and in the United Kingdom by
FirstForumPress
A division of Lynne Rienner Publishers, Inc.
3 Henrietta Street, Covent Garden, London WC2E 8LU

Library of Congress Cataloging-in-Publication Data
Balboni, Jennifer M.
  Clergy sexual abuse litigation : survivors seeking justice /
Jennifer M. Balboni.
  Includes bibliographical references and index.
  ISBN 978-1-935049-37-1 (hardcover : alk. paper)
  1. Child sexual abuse by clergy—United States. 2. Actions and defenses—
United States. 3. Liability for child sexual abuse—United States. 4. Catholic
Church—Clergy—Sexual behavior. 5. Clergy—Sexual behavior—United States.
6. Children—Legal status, laws, etc.—United States. I. Title.
KF1328.5.C45B35 2011
345.73'0253—dc22   2011000743

British Cataloguing in Publication Data
A Cataloguing in Publication record for this book
is available from the British Library.

This book was produced from digital files prepared by the author
using the FirstForumComposer.

Printed and bound in the United States of America

∞   The paper used in this publication meets the requirements
     of the American National Standard for Permanence of
     Paper for Printed Library Materials Z39.48-1992.

5 4 3 2 1

Contents

Acknowledgments

To my husband and family for walking with me through this unimaginable journey: Your patience, faith, and support made this work possible.

To Donna Bishop, the most dedicated and supportive mentor anyone could ever hope for: I thank you.

Most important, to the survivors and their advocates: I thank you. Your courage can move mountains.

***

Portions of Chapter 5 previously appeared in a somewhat different form as "Transformative Justice: Survivor Perspectives on Clergy Sexual Abuse Litigation," coauthored by Jennifer M. Balboni and Donna M. Bishop in *Contemporary Justice Review*, 13, pp. 133-154. Used by permission of the publisher.

You were once in darkness,
but now you are light in the Lord.
Live as children of the light, for light
produces every kind of goodness, righteousness, and truth.

—Ephesians 5:8-9,
Revised New American Bible

1
Introduction

George[1] is a middle-aged, single man, a survivor of clergy sexual abuse spanning several years when he was a child into adolescence. He has moved many times in his life, and worked sporadically. Like many other survivors, he could not find the words to tell his family about what was happening to him during the time it occurred, although he bitterly states that his acting out behaviors should have signaled red flags to his family that he was being abused. When George disclosed as an adult, people who knew him would comment frequently that they had some idea that the priest molested children—"fiddling and diddling"— as some put it. These admissions, he tells me, may have been more painful than the actual abuse. At points, he reports that he has been filled with rage that no one intervened to help him or the other children, and that adults blithely turned their heads, tacitly acknowledging what was happening when they remarked, "There goes Father X on his ice cream run." It is that indifference, perpetrated not only by those in the community, but also particularly by officials within the Church, that is at once baffling and painful to him.

As an adult, George initially called the Church in hopes that it would pay for therapy, which it initially did. After a few months of therapy, however, the funding was terminated. "At that point in healing, you're standing on the edge of a cliff; you're looking into an abyss that threatens to kill you. You can commit suicide at any point in your therapy, because you've done some work, you're ready to do deeper work." At this point, he started writing the Church, petitioning it to continue paying for his therapy, a mostly unsuccessful campaign that would ultimately drag on for years. With each refusal to pay and brush off, he tells me he felt re-wounded by the Church. He joined litigation only after another denial, where a Church representative suggested to him that if he was unhappy with their decision he could hire a lawyer—a challenge which he took.

When I ask him whether litigation did what he set out to accomplish, his answer is enlightening and captures what many survivors might feel about litigation being beside the point:

> "What I wanted to accomplish? I don't even look at it in those terms. [laughs] Surviving … Trying to survive … You try to get through a day [laughs] without turning to booze or drugs or a gun to [your] head or whatever escape that people use … Because I [at points] considered it … a journey within to my own wholeness and healing my broken heart, or my own woundedness … I wouldn't use the word 'accomplishment'—I would use 'fulfillment', some sense of harmony or peace or acceptance might be used. So, when I finished the settlement, because I was speaking from that place, and I was living from that place, there was a sense of healing. Stepping into that vulnerability again and healing. So whether I got 50 bucks or 500,000 bucks, it's all part of a bigger picture that is kind of a sidebar to the journey, to the real journey."

George's journey morphed many times during the course of litigation. At points, it was about getting therapy paid for; at other points, it was about making the Church tell the truth about its role in the abuse. At still other moments, it was about healing, or perhaps even getting revenge. For many clergy sexual abuse survivors, motivations were often a moving target.

In some respects, George was lucky. He came to see the litigation as one way to rebuild his life—not through money or settlement, but by assigning responsibility and unloading the pain of his past. Many other survivors didn't fare nearly as well.

Survivors Seeking Justice

As I write this in the summer of 2010, stories of Catholic clergy sexually abusing children with tacit approval by a complicit hierarchy have once again bubbled up in the international media. The stories are familiar; only the geography has changed: priests who preyed on children, warnings that went unheeded, and lives irrevocably changed. By now, with new reports from Ireland, Germany, and Australia, (Gilgoff 2010) it is abundantly clear to most people that the Catholic hierarchy not only allowed this type of systemic abuse to occur, but also in many cases, the hierarchy's benign neglect permitted this abuse to flourish.

To be very clear, sexual predators exist in every occupation. They are teachers, ministers, scout masters, accountants; they exist in all walks of life. What makes this story different is that in the Catholic

Church, these people were harbored in ways that other organizations were unable or unwilling to do. Although members of the Church have issued different apologies over the last decade, real accountability—via the criminal justice system—is often out of reach in these cases. This leaves much of the business of justice to the realm of civil litigation.

While these stories may present "more of the same" of what the American public has now come to accept, this awareness was not always so widespread. When I began my research in 2003, the realization that thousands of children were routinely ignored by the Catholic Church hierarchy was very new. Many Catholics—including myself—found themselves lost trying to understand how such incredible disregard could have happened by men charged with managing the Church. The linchpin for this shift in understanding was the civil litigation that more than 550 survivors in Boston initiated in 2002. What happened then changed the rules of engagement for not only survivors of abuse and leaders of the Church, but also for Catholic laity as well.

Although many lawsuits had been filed in prior years, through 2001 the litigation generally centered around one or two serial sex offenders and most often resulted in settlements that included secrecy clauses that isolated and separated victims and minimized media attention. In contrast, the litigation explosion that ensued in 2002 involved multiple perpetrators, victims, dioceses, and countries. Furthermore, the settlements did not include provisions that hushed victims into silent submission. These events proved pivotal in the world's understanding of the Church's role in the abuse. Survivors around the globe now disclose to a different cultural audience than they did a decade ago; they may find more acceptance and be believed more often than they had in the past. This is due in no small part to the litigation that took place in 2002, primarily in Boston. Most major news outlets in America and Europe have covered this crisis repeatedly, and most have done so with some empathy toward survivors and with a critical eye toward the Church which not only failed to stop the abuse, but also knowingly put reputed sex offenders in contact with thousands of children. The impact of this litigation cannot be underestimated.

Still, while this litigation was immensely consequential, its impact on those involved has yet to be fully understood. Reflecting on the impact of the clergy sexual abuse scandal, leading child abuse researcher David Finkelhor writes:

> … One of the topics this scandal has raised and which deserves much more discussion in the child maltreatment field is the role of lawsuits and litigation. There is no doubt that the plaintiffs' attorneys played a

heroic leadership role in bringing this issue to the fore and forcing the crucial disclosures that allowed the scope of the problem to be appreciated fully. Many of the victims might have never come forward without the support of these attorneys ... But their activities raise some questions ... The process of litigation on behalf of survivors has not been subjected to the same kind of scrutiny that say, police investigators, child welfare investigators or mental health providers have received. For example, how are the plaintiffs recruited? What kinds of informed consent procedures are undertaken with them? What are the traumatizing portions of the litigation process, and how are these stresses managed and mitigated? ... It definitely signals the need for more scrutiny of the process and best practice standards for civil litigation. It signals the need for more study about the impact of this process on survivors, their families and their recovery process (2003, p. 1226).

The research presented in this book attempts to answer some of these questions, and conveys the survivors' back-stories, which received much less attention from the media.

When I set out in my research, I wanted to qualitatively understand why so many victims had waited so long to come forward and what they were trying to achieve. Were they interested in retribution? Reconciliation? Restitution? And why had so many victims chosen civil litigation over other alternatives? Did life go on as usual during the litigation, or was the suit a catalyst for important life changes? This research chronicles why survivors litigated, and it speaks to some of the theoretical and practical debates about motivations in civil litigation. It also examines what survivors accomplished through that litigation, and how litigation sometimes transformed pieces of their lives.

The second chapter will explore the history and context of clergy sexual abuse within the Catholic Church. This section outlines the long history of sexual abuse by priests and the Church's response to it; it also provides a context with which to understand this type of abuse. I detail how a constellation of taboos makes this abuse particularly complex and consequential for survivors. I have also tried to frame the litigation within larger societal shifts (e.g., victim advocacy, Catholic doctrine), as well as note the historical implications of this litigation. Finally, the last section of this chapter outlines the interdisciplinary theoretical foundation which guided this research; the research is grounded in the law and society tradition, but is complemented with theoretical perspectives from victimology, psychology, and justice studies.

Chapter Three delves immediately into the rich tapestry that the survivors wove about who they are. It details what the survivors had in common, as well as their differences, and examines their complicated relationship with the Church. Chapters Four, Five, Six, Seven and Eight walk through the process of litigation from the survivors' perspectives, from disclosure of the abuse to initiating litigation and finally through settlement. These accounts provide powerful testament to the complexity of this type of litigation, examining its successes and failures. Finally, in the last chapter, I try to summarize what can be learned from these survivors' journeys, including the mistakes that were made and the victories that were won.

I must caution the reader that although I did interview attorneys and other legal advocates, the focus of this book is *clergy sexual abuse survivors in the civil justice system*, not legal strategy or ethics. Although I do make some recommendations about legal practices that particularly helped or hindered survivors, I do so primarily based upon what the survivors shared with me, with significant input from experts in the field.

My sense at the outset of this research was that the litigation wasn't about the money. This book is about what it really meant to survivors— what their conceptions of justice were, and whether they achieved them. I have tried to bear as truthful a witness as possible to the meaning of this litigation for survivors. I am honored they shared their stories with me.

---

[1] All names of the survivors, advocates, offenders, and Church officials have been changed.

2
Clergy Sexual Abuse:
Historical and Theoretical Context

In this chapter, I've tried to create an interdisciplinary primer of sorts on the topic of clergy sexual abuse and its corresponding litigation. The review that follows discusses clergy sexual abuse and its historical treatment in the Catholic Church both before and after the litigation explosion of 2002, as well as provides a theoretical background for the study. The chapter is organized into five sections. The first two sections discuss clergy sexual abuse in the Catholic Church from the early Church through the twentieth century and the literature on clergy sexual abuse to date. The third section focuses on precursors to the 2002 litigation, with a focus on shifts in social awareness, theology, and litigation in the decades preceding the sexual abuse scandal of 2002. The fourth section details the clergy sexual abuse scandal of 2002 and its historical impact on the present day. Finally, the last section will discuss the theoretical work that grounds this study in the law and society genre.

Historical Background of Clergy Sexual Abuse

In part due to the highly taboo nature of the topic, clergy sexual abuse has been subject to less scrutiny than other types of abuse. Access to data and records has been exceedingly difficult to obtain (Burroughs 1992): the Catholic Church has been a veritable black hole of information. Though case records exist, often they have been sealed in Vatican archives (Bruni and Burkett 2002, p. 28). For many centuries, priests were exempt from civil law, and allegations of clergy sexual abuse were handled in secret ecclesiastic tribunals. Victims were frequently disbelieved or blamed for the events, which had a chilling effect on disclosures. Still, despite recent assertions by members of the Church hierarchy that they either did not know about the problem or did not understand its deleterious effects, records of the phenomenon have existed for centuries. Moreover, for the past few decades, the United

States Council of Catholic Bishops (USCCB) has been involved in ongoing discussion and debate both about the problem of clergy sexual abuse and about how best to shield the Church's own documentation of the problem from outside scrutiny (Bruni and Burkett 2002).

Although pederasty (sexual contact between adult men and young boys) has roots that predate the early Church, historical reports reveal a familiar, if intermittent, problem with clergy sexual abuse dating back to 305 A.D., when the Council of Elvira prohibited "corrupters of boys" from receiving communion (Isley 1997). Church documents reveal that pederasty became a concern once again in the tenth and eleventh centuries, when it was acknowledged that the practice of "child oblation" (surrendering one's son for monastic preparation) facilitated clergy sexual predation. Isley writes:

> St. Basil, a Benedictine monk, issued strict penalties on adult treatment of children in monasteries and his writings show great concern about the sexual attraction of an adult towards his young male pupils. This appears justified, moreover, considering the number of documents in which the tenth and eleventh century monks wrote love poems celebrating "Paederastia" (1997, p. 280).

In fact, a fairly elaborate punishment scheme was enacted by the monks for sexual contact between monks and oblates. However, while the Church considered pederasty inappropriate and offensive, blame was usually assigned to both the cleric and the child, regardless of the child's age or lack of consent (Isley 1997).

The idea of shared responsibility, however, did not enjoy unanimous support. Father Peter Damian, a Benedictine monk in the eleventh century and later a canonized saint, condemned pederasty as "spiritual infanticide." Rather than assigning blame to the children, Damian saw the clergy as wholly responsible. Moreover, Damian was critical not only of clergy molesters, but also of their superiors who failed to take decisive action to prevent the acts. He wrote prolifically on "the sexual immorality of the clergy and the laxness of superiors who refused to take a strong hand against it" (Isley 1997). Although Damian's treatise was accepted by Pope Leo IX, his strong recommendations to remove all offending clerics from ministry were not embraced (Weigel 2002). Instead, the Pope took a decidedly more lenient tack: only those clerics who had offended multiple times were excluded from clerical life (Doyle 2003), a move consistent with the Vatican's response in the early twenty-first century.

Sexual contact between clerics and children was the subject of renewed attention in the fifteenth and sixteenth centuries, when several monks and their child victims were publicly punished. Following these accounts, the Council of Trent (1545-1563) issued two canons that discussed sexual activity by clerics. Although pederasty was not specifically mentioned, scholars generally accept that the notations were aimed specifically at clergy sexual abuse of children (Doyle 2003). The current Code of Canon Law defines sexual contact with a minor by a cleric as a crime (c. 1395, as quoted in Doyle 2003). Aside from several well-chronicled examples of priests being publicly flogged or punished for sexual contact with children, little was written about pederasty from the Middle Ages to the modern era, perhaps because the Church kept a tight lid on information and processed infractions in secret tribunals (Bruni and Burkett 2002).

Clergy sexual abuse of children was again recognized as a problem in the modern Church, forced in part by allegations and corresponding civil and criminal filings against Father Gilbert Gauthe in Louisiana in the 1980s. Although lawsuits like this had occurred previously, this case received national media coverage, breaking the unspoken but well recognized pact by the media to leave Church matters alone. Perhaps as a result of the negative publicity around this case and several others, the Church commissioned a panel to investigate the extent of the problem. The panel produced a report entitled "The Problem of Sexual Molestation by Roman Catholic Clergy: Meeting the Problem in a Comprehensive and Responsible Manner" (Mouton, Doyle, and Peterson 1985), which chronicled the history of modern reports of clergy sexual abuse in this country, citing nearly thirty cases that had been reported in the press—usually only the local press—involving approximately 100 children. The authors speculated that if the problem was not tackled proactively, with swift inpatient treatment for offending priests and pastoral responses to the victims, it could mushroom, eventually costing the Church upwards of $1 billion in settlement costs, legal fees, and counseling expenses. The authors suggested a protocol that included assigning skilled and empathic liaisons for parents, and pulling priests credibly accused out of ministry for the safety of the general public. They also warned that major news sources were beginning to follow the story, and that bishops could no longer count on a deferential media to pass on potential stories (Mouton et al. 1985). Much to the authors' surprise, when the Mouton et al. report was released, its confidentiality was secured, as only a limited number of copies were published, and the warnings contained therein were largely ignored by much of the Church hierarchy for many years (Doyle, personal communication November 2004)[1].

In 1985, Attorney Jeffrey Anderson of Minnesota filed another successful lawsuit against the Catholic Church alleging clergy sexual abuse (Jenkins 1997). In earlier eras, litigating against the Catholic Church was grounds for excommunication under canon law. Unquestionably, the success of Anderson's case regarding Father Adamson, as well as the Gauthe case, opened a door of opportunity for survivors.

After this round of settlements in the late 1980s, the Vatican began to take notice. In 1990, Bishop A. James Quinn told a seminar of Church leaders and lawyers that if they were worried about any documents that contained damning information about sexual abuse allegations, they should shuttle the documents out of the diocese to the "apostolic delegate" in Washington D.C., which has full immunity (Gibson 2003, p. 40). Other hardball maneuvers to fend off the growing threat of litigation included countersuits against victims and the hiring of private investigators to search for information that might discredit an alleged victim's character (Gibson 2003).

Just a few years later, in 1993, another scandal erupted following allegations of sexual abuse by Father James Porter in Fall River, Massachusetts. In response, the National Conference of Catholic Bishops (NCCB) acknowledged clergy sexual abuse as a "serious problem" and developed a series of policies to address it. These policies included requiring:

A prompt and thorough investigation by the Church into any allegation of abuse,

Spiritual and psychological assistance for the victim and his or her family,

Protection of the rights of the accused, and

Appropriate notification to the parish involved (O'Connor 1993, p. 315).

However, under the structure of the NCCB, there is no duty to obey such protocol; the bishops are not beholden to anyone but the Holy See (the Pope).

The topic of clergy sexual abuse again made the Bishops' agenda in 1993, 1994, and 1995, when a "think tank" of experts in child sexual abuse, commissioned by the Bishops, sent urgent messages regarding the need to respond pastorally: "... [We] are concerned that the hierarchy's authority and credibility in the United States is eroding ..." (Rossetti 1996, p. 15). This body further distributed informational packets to the bishops about the consequences of abuse and the need for "restoring trust" (Rossetti 1996, pp. 15-16). Still, the Vatican characterized the problem in some statements as one that was largely "American" (Rossetti 1996, pp. 16-17), and shifted blame to the media. For instance, during the Porter scandal, Cardinal Law famously invoked "God's power down on the media, particularly the [*Boston*] *Globe*," stating that "the media like to focus on the faults of the few" (Gibson 2003, p. 4).

At the same time, Pope John Paul II noted that the problem could be attributed in part to selection processes for candidates for the priesthood (Rossetti 1996). As a result, significant changes were made in the screening process at seminaries, with the hope that emotionally immature or psychologically unstable men would be filtered out of the seminary before ever getting in (Weigel 2002). However, despite these reforms and all of the dire predictions, responses by bishops varied considerably. Some responded pastorally (e.g., Joseph Bernardin in Chicago apologized publicly on several occasions and implemented inclusive lay boards of oversight with victim representation and a publicized hotline [Steinfels 2003, p. 48; Jenkins 1996]). Others provided little more than window dressing in an attempt to maintain business as usual. Moreover, the discussion about sexual abuse generally characterized the behavior as a sin rather than a crime against society.

Over the next few years, the slow bloodletting of litigation continued across the country, usually involving one or two chronic pedophiles as the center of controversy with dozens of victims surfacing. Typically, these suits involved "no talk" clauses—enforceable because they were included as part of a larger settlement package—that stifled widespread or enduring media coverage. The Church's strategy up through 2002 was largely one of "containment" (Rossetti 1996, p. 22). Perhaps as a result, images of clergy sexual abuse were "largely disconnected" around the country (Jenkins 1996). During these early stages of litigation, awareness about sexual abuse and its consequences generally—as well as clergy sexual abuse specifically—was building.

Phenomenological Features of Clergy Sexual Abuse

Despite the long, albeit disconnected, documented history of clergy sexual abuse, there was very little empirical inquiry into the subject. Although the litigation in 2002 spurred on a great deal of interest, up to that point, scholarly inquiry was usually limited to anecdotal information and case studies. This body of work suggests that clergy sexual abuse is similar to other types of sexual abuse in many aspects, yet also distinct in important ways. For instance, a victim's age, gender, family background, choice of audience for disclosure, and level of violence involved in the incident are all relevant variables when considering the impact of all types of sexual abuse[2]. Other aspects of clergy sexual abuse, however, present different phenomenological features from other types of sexual abuse. First, clergy sexual abuse cases are unique in that they do not fit neatly into the category of either intra- or extra-familial abuse. Anecdotal evidence presented in various journalistic accounts strongly suggests that clergy sexual abuse shares many psychological and interpersonal dynamics with incest (Benyei 1998; deFuentes 1999; Fortune 1990; Schoener and Milgrom 1990), so much so, in fact, that clinicians may use this framework in treating clergy sexual abuse victims. Dr. Mary Gail Frawley O'Dea, a clinical specialist who works with clergy sexual abuse victims, asserts:

> The sexual violation of a child or adolescent by a priest is, in fact, incest. It is a sexual and relationship betrayal perpetrated by the father of the child's extended family: a man in whom the child is—or was— taught from birth onward to trust above everyone else in his life, to trust second only to God (2004, p. 18).

In many of the accounts of clergy sexual abuse, the priest had become an ad hoc member of the victim's family. In some cases, priests even had their own rooms in the victim's home, vacationed with the family (Investigative Staff of *The Boston Globe* 2002, p. 89), or routinely prayed with and told bedtime stories to the children (p. 15, 82). Additionally, there are numerous accounts of priests acting *in loco parentis* by maintaining positions of leadership in alternative settings for youth, such as boarding schools (Harris 1990) or homes for troubled adolescents (Investigative Staff 2002, p. 74). Moreover, to state an obvious point, the priest is referred to as "Father" by members of the community.

Although the priest is usually not a biological family member, the Church community is often portrayed as a family (Cooper-White 1991; Gaylor 1988), and the priest functions as a guardian not only to the child, but also to the child's parents. In short, the amount of trust usually associated with the priest, the secrecy involved, and the potential family disruption if disclosed, all seem more consistent with intra-familial abuse. Gaylor notes:

> Consider, if you will, the impact on a child [who] is sexually abused during the week, and on Sundays witnesses his parents bowing, kneeling, genuflecting, praying and receiving sacraments and graciously thanking the priest for his involvement in their lives (1988, p. 14).

A victim explains:

> You've got God. You've got priests. Then you've got your parents. Then yourself. I couldn't turn to my mother because Father Gauthe was above my mother (Bruni and Burkett 2002, p. 101).

This dynamic, then, appears to transcend the prototypical incest, since priests are often regarded as more powerful than the actual parents. The implications of this may be profound.

These dynamics may be so powerful that the victim may not be able to reconcile what has happened in secret with the public persona of the priest. Psychologist and priest Stephen Rossetti argues: "The reality of clergy sexual misconduct is resisted even by the victims" (1996, p. 28). One man, abused by a priest at twelve, states, "... I wasn't sure this was really happening to me" (Rossetti 1996, p. 28). Father Canice Connors, longtime head of St. Luke's Treatment Center for sexually offending priests, states, "We must be aware that the child sometimes retains a loving memory of the offender" (Bruni and Burkett 2002, p. 41). In a speech addressing the Bishops' Council in 2003, one victim described the complex relationship between himself and his abuser, "The most amazing part ... [was] when I allowed [myself] to talk about my abuser [and] how this man offered kindness and love; how this man became [my] friend" (Gibson 2003, p. 29). Because of the closeness of the priest to the family, the role that he holds in the community, and the Catholic theology that anoints the priest as God's chosen representative, the child victim may have difficulty acknowledging acts of sexual predation as abusive.

Under these circumstances, simply ignoring abusive events or labeling them as something else may be preferable to believing or understanding that this "chosen" man has done something so wrong. Considering these conditions of the relationship between a priest and a child, the child may have difficulty identifying or naming the experience as abusive, which is typically the first stage in any transformation of disputes (Felstiner, Abel, and Sarat 1980-1981).

The centrality of religion in the context of the abuse may be the most singularly unique dimension of clergy sexual abuse. The role of the priest in Catholic theology is crucial to this understanding. Priests have special status as representatives of God. Catholic dogma dictates that the priest is an *"alter Christus"*—"another Christ" (Weigel 2002, p. 40); during ordination, priests "assume the person of Christ" (p. 23). This ultimately means that victims are being betrayed not only by a highly-revered, trusted individual, but also by someone with an otherworldly, semi-divine status.

The priest's duties include intercession for the layperson to God (deFuentes 1999). In Mass, it is the priest who literally speaks the Word of God through the Gospel, and—perhaps most importantly for Catholics—it is the priest who has the power to transubstantiate the bread and wine into the Body and Blood of Christ, which, according to Catholic doctrine, is the source of redemption and forgiveness. Additionally, the priest is the only person who has sacramental powers: the power to baptize children into God's kingdom; the power to forgive sins, thereby controlling access to eternal salvation; and the power to observe and sanctify a marriage. Religious scholar and outspoken critic Father Tom Doyle cogently summarizes the priest's authority: "Sacraments are also the key moments in the life path of Catholics. The Church teaches that the sacraments are the source of holiness and the means to salvation for Catholics" (2003, p. 218). In this way, the priest is the observable portal to God.

Considering this, it is perhaps not surprising that individuals abused by clergy reported excessive amounts of self-blame (Disch and Avery 2001; Schoener and Milgrom 1990). Victims often feel that their sinfulness has led a "pure" clergyman of the highest virtue to fall from grace (Schoener and Milgrom 1990, p. 229), thus providing another powerful incentive not to disclose the abuse. Even if the survivor is able to name the experience as "injurious" or abusive, they may have distinct problems with assigning blame, the second stage in the transformation of disputes (Felstiner et al. 1980-1981). "Victims may feel that they must have been really bad, since this holy, God-like person singled them out for abuse" (Horst 1998, p. 24). Further, they feel hopeless in believing that they are, "... so wicked, God couldn't possibly forgive them, that they are deeply flawed and likely to contaminate others ..." (p. 23). According to Pamela Cooper-White, a clinician working with female victims of clergy sexual abuse, victims often feel that, in effect, their souls have been stolen (1991, p. 196). The terror that accompanies this fear, she asserts, is almost incomprehensible to non-victims; it essentially means spiritual death for the victim: utter hopelessness (Cooper-White 1996).

In addition, Catholic dogma also has very specific implications for disclosure in clergy sexual abuse cases. The laity are taught deference and obedience toward priests' and bishops' authority through a class system: "bishop above priest, priest above common man, man above woman, adult above child" (Bruni and Burkett 2002, p. 61). Bruni and Burkett (2002) note that priests, in particular, are held up even higher than other clergypersons. Tim Martinez, raped by a priest in his home, states, "You just can't go around saying a priest did something wrong in a community where priests almost walk on water" (Bruni and Burkett 2004, p. 67). Such a system suggests an almost irresistible dynamic, ensuring that victims remain silent.

With these considerations in mind about the context of clergy sexual abuse, concurrent societal changes, discussed below, laid the groundwork for the Church sex scandal that began in 2002.

Precursors to the 2002 Watershed

As has been discussed here, the problem of clergy sexual abuse was recognized in certain circles in the 1980s and 1990s, but many felt that the scandal had already come and gone. For instance, in 1997, Church historian Charles Morris wrote:

> Some hundreds of priests have been identified as child sexual abusers, the worst of whom were predatory monsters who victimized dozens, even hundreds of children—James Porter in Massachusetts, Thomas Adamson in Minnesota ... Legal settlements have been expensive; the diocese of Albuquerque contemplated filing for bankruptcy because of the sexual abuse claims ... (p. 292). [However, the] pedophilia scandals finally appear to be winding down, and there are reasons to hope that dioceses have learned valuable lessons about honesty and about the consequences of pretending not to see catastrophes that are staring you in the face
> (p. 294).

Sadly, Morris couldn't have been more wrong. He did not count on several key shifts in the macro environment that helped light the wick that would become the explosion of litigation in 2002, the first of which involved changes within the Church itself.

The Second Vatican Council

Ironically, some of the most important shifts on the political horizon involved changes the Catholic Church had made several decades earlier. Following what may have been the crest of popular support for the Vatican amongst American Catholics (Perko 1989), the Second Vatican Council (Vatican II) was undertaken from 1962-1965 to examine "the structure of the Church and assess its relationship to the modern world" (O'Connor 1998, p. 236). Only the third time such a Council had been convened (the first was the Council of Trent in 1545, the second was the First Vatican Council in 1869), the Council focused *inter alia* on the laity's role in the Church[3]. The major Catholic religious ceremony—the Mass—shifted from the "Roman Rite" in Latin to the vernacular to bring the message to congregants in a direct and personal way (Perko 1989). Lay persons became more active in the Mass as lectors and Eucharistic ministers; parish councils sprang up to assist with both financial and spiritual governance. Prior to this time, most people prayed in silence as the Mass went on in a foreign language (Perko 1989). For the first time, the priest faced the congregation during Mass, as opposed to celebrating with his back to the people (Muller 2003, p. 219). In short, the laity were invited to participate in both religious rites and Church governance.

The following passages from Vatican II express this shift from rigid hierarchy to reciprocity in the relationship between the Church and its people:

> ... the Constitution teaches that there is a mutual relationship of support and dependence between laity and clergy (Vatican II: Dogmatic Constitution on the Church, *Lumen Gentium* 1962-1965, p. 32).

> [The laity] are, by [reason of] knowledge, competence or outstanding ability which they may enjoy, permitted and sometimes even obliged to express their opinion on those things which concern the good of the Church (p. 37).

Such discussion about lay members of the Church was revolutionary within the Catholic Church at that time.

Despite the progressive mandates about the relationship between the Church and the laity, once the substantial changes in the Mass occurred, the laity found themselves locked out of higher order church functioning; any ideas anyone might have had about the Church becoming more democratic were quickly quashed. Critical or alternative interpretations of the Bible were unwelcome. Despite the attempt to engage the laity, the subsequent leadership at the Vatican—especially Pope John Paul II—reinforced the hierarchical nature of the Church and the importance and power of the clergy (O'Connor 1998). In fact, despite the appearance of becoming more modern, some critics point to the period immediately post Vatican II as particularly monarchical in terms of Catholic teaching (Kung 2003). Soon after the legislation in Vatican II was announced, *Humanae Vitae* was issued. It put forth a definitive Church position banning artificial contraception as immoral, which set off incredible discord between the clergy and the laity in the United States. Similar conservative positions were issued on homosexuality, divorce, euthanasia, and abortion, prompting further dissent.

In addition to discussing the role of the laity, Vatican II reinforced the importance of the priest. Historian George Weigel (2002) writes:

> Vatican II taught another venerable truth: that ordained priests are "living instruments of Christ the eternal priest." At his ordination, every priest "assumes the person of Christ." The Catholic priest, in other words, is not simply a religious functionary, a man licensed to do certain kinds of ecclesiastical business. A Catholic priest is an icon, a living re-presentation, of the eternal priesthood of Jesus Christ. He makes the Christ present in the Church in a singular way, by acting in persona Christi, "in the person of Christ," at the altar and in administering the sacraments. The Catholic priesthood, in other words, is not just another form of ministry. Ordination to the priesthood in the Catholic Church radically transforms who the man is, not just what he does (p. 25).

The authoritative text on Catholic dogma, *Catechism of the Catholic Church,* lays out the doctrine that explains the immense power of a priest:

> This sacrament configures the recipient to Christ by a special grace of the Holy Spirit, so that he may serve as Christ's instrument for his Church. By ordination one is enabled to act as a representative ... (p. 1581).

> The sacrament of the Holy Orders ... confers an *indelible spiritual character* and cannot be repeated or conferred temporarily (p. 1582).

The role of the priest as living representation of Christ, then, was reinforced during the reforms of the sixties. Despite more lay involvement on other fronts, the priest remained the only figure who could forgive a person's sins, who could give last rites to the dying, or who could perform a baptism. And, most important of all, the priest remained the only person empowered to perform the Eucharistic sacrifice, a ceremony wherein Catholics believe bread and wine are transformed into the Body and Blood of Jesus Christ. This ceremony, a reenactment of the Last Supper, is the heart of Catholicism. Doctrinally it is seen as the source of redemption for Catholics, the "food of eternal life" (*Catechism of the Catholic Church* 1994, p. 1212). These facets of the "eternal priesthood" were reaffirmed and upheld through Vatican II, alongside the more progressive missives about the laity.

As a result of some of the confusion over the directions signaled by Vatican II and several conservative positions taken by the Church on social issues, Catholic historian Hans Kung notes that in the last quarter of the twentieth century "an unprecedented process of the erosion of Church authority" took place, with an expanding divide between the "church from above" and the "church from below" (2003, pp. 197-198). Historian Charles Morris described the situation as dire and observed that "The Church is ripped with theological dissensus" (1997, p. 293).

So the changes both within the Church and between the hierarchy and the laity laid the groundwork for the scandal of 2002. Even though many of the more inviting doctrines of Vatican II had effectively become dead letters in the three decades that followed, the seeds of change had already taken root, and a revolution of rising expectations had begun to gather momentum. The Church would soon learn this was a difficult bell to un-ring.

Social Awareness

Another major force shaping the public response to allegations of clergy sexual abuse was a shift in public awareness about sexual abuse (Jenkins 1996). This awareness contributed to the victims' rights movement of the 1980s, which provided both a language (Dunn 2010) and a philosophical platform from which victims could demand justice. Several key things were accomplished through this movement: first, it posited that being a victim was not shameful, and second, it made the consequences of victimization clearer. Criminal justice agencies, as well as the larger society, came to understand the effects of victimization. Newly recognized as a condition that sprang from exposure to traumatic events (e.g., child abuse, combat in war), Post Traumatic Stress Disorder (PTSD) was added to the American Psychological Association's *Diagnostic and Statistical Manual of Mental Disorders*. Further, the victims' rights movement specifically promoted awareness about child abuse, particularly child sexual abuse. The 1980s saw a proliferation of empirical studies of child abuse and its consequences.

On the legislative front, by the late 1970s most states expanded earlier mandatory reporting laws to include more personnel who interacted with children. By the late nineties, more than half of the states still allowed for "clergy-penitent" exceptions to the mandatory reporting laws, although these were usually not expressly stipulated in the law (Pudelski 2004). Still, by 2002, in most states the privilege had significantly eroded to interaction limited to the confessional. In short, society's tolerance for failure to act on behalf of victims of child abuse was exceedingly slim.

Information Availability

Finally, in the decade leading up to the Church sex scandal in 2002, the internet blossomed into a medium of global information. Although the internet was available in 1992 when earlier clergy sexual abuse crises occurred (e.g., involving Father Porter), it had not yet transformed the way people communicated. The information revolution would prove to be a key piece in blowing what could have been a Boston scandal to international proportions.

Finally, the media's coverage of violent and sexual content shifted. Religious historian and journalist Peter Steinfels divides the media coverage into "pre-Lewinsky" and "post-Lewinsky" periods, noting that previously understated sexual details were no longer off limits (2003, p. 45). These shifts in social awareness, legislation, and media coverage would prove consequential in the scandal of 2002.

These pre-conditions—the work done through Vatican II in re-conceptualizing the role of the laity, the proliferation of the internet, the work done in victims' rights, and the information revolution—laid the groundwork necessary for the impending socio-legal crisis of 2002. But more than the sum of these parts, the soil in Boston proved wildly fertile for dissent against the Catholic hierarchy. The greater Boston area, known for both its intellectualism and rebellious spirit, is home to more than two million Catholics. Although the Church had been a key player in nearly every major historical event in the city in the last century, in 2002, rather than helping to negotiate challenges outside the Church (e.g., the Boston bussing crisis, violent abortion protests, or living wages for workers), the Church would find itself at the center of its own scandal.

The Sexual Abuse Scandal of 2002 and Beyond

In 2001, two of the most powerful entities in Boston clashed over access to Church files. Prompted by litigation against the Archdiocese involving defrocked priest John Geoghan, *The Boston Globe* began its own investigation into the way the Church hierarchy had responded to the pedophilic priest. After months of legal wrangling, the *Globe* successfully pried previously confidential personal and legal documents from the Archdiocese, citing that "public interest outweighed privacy concerns of the litigants" (Investigative Staff 2002, p. xi). Although Geoghan was accused of abuse by more than one hundred people, the most striking aspect of the unraveling story involved Geoghan's repeated reassignment into new parishes after fresh allegations of abuse were made. Documents indicated that the Cardinal had been aware of Geoghan's offenses since 1984, but waited nearly twelve years to remove him from active duty. Even then, no sanctions were imposed; instead, he was placed on "senior priest retirement status." Without question, the linchpin in breaking the scandal of 2002 involved the declassification of these Archdiocesan documents.

The story was published in early January 2002, coinciding with the public criminal trial of Father Geoghan on charges listed in indictments issued in late 1999. Only weeks after the initial report, Geoghan was found guilty of indecent assault and battery for improperly touching a ten-year-old boy in 1992. Stating the high probability of recidivism and Geoghan's utter lack of remorse or acceptance of personal responsibility, the judge sentenced him to the maximum sentence of nine to ten years in prison[4]. The trial provided a very public, dramatic morality play about the sexually assaultive behavior of one priest. Although the Church itself was not on trial for its complicity, the spotlight brought the actions of both Geoghan and his superiors onto the front stage. Perhaps one result of this trial was shifting the language of the crisis from "sin" to "crime."

Just days after the trial ended, the *Globe* ran another top-of-the-fold story chronicling a decade of behind-the-scenes sexual abuse litigation involving more than seventy priests in the Archdiocese. The article solidified many Catholics' worst fears: that the earlier accusations weren't aberrations, and that clergy sexual abuse was a serious problem within the Archdiocese. Worse still, the files indicated a clear modus operandi of secrecy, limited or no treatment, and reassignment (i.e., geographic solutions) for accused priests, with no system of automatic notification to criminal justice agencies. Further, the Church had placed concern for its own reputation above the safety of its youngest members.

Perhaps most significantly, most incidents of abuse had been previously shielded from the public eye through confidentiality clauses and no-talk rules, apparently implemented to preserve the confidentiality of priests and to silence victims. Interestingly, the story of the crisis within the Church caught fire with little reference to the longstanding, if scattered, history of clergy sexual abuse.

Nearly a week after Geoghan's conviction, another priest, Father Paquin, admitted in a media interview that he had sexually abused young boys over the course of two decades. Soon after, the Archdiocese suspended six priests. At this point, the Attorney General (AG) became involved and forced the Boston Archdiocese to release the names of victims over the previous sixty years, once again grounding the discussion of clergy sexual abuse in the secular world of "crime" rather than "sin." The AG's inquiry questioned whether criminal charges would be possible or appropriate, which prompted a discussion about both the fairness of statutory limitations for sex crimes in general and about clergy exemptions from mandatory reporting laws[5]. Over the next year, dozens of local priests became implicated in the scandal.

It is unclear whether there was a clear trigger for the avalanche of victims who subsequently came forward to sue the Archdiocese, but the events of March 2002 indisputably had some effect. At that time, several more victims came forward to implicate Monsignor Fred Ryan, the highest ranking priest to be accused of sexual abuse at that time. Around the same time, accounts of sexual abuse by Father Joseph Birmingham began to gain momentum. In April 2002, Attorney Roderick MacLeish and several of his Birmingham-affiliated clients held a press conference to release nearly 1,000 pages of archdiocesan files on clergy sexual abuse. The conference was covered—uninterrupted—by all the major media networks in Boston, and was later looped by nearly every national major news organization. The Boston Catholic Church's response to abuse was being challenged, and its credibility began to spiral (Paulson 2002).

By the end of April 2002, the exposure of clergy sexual abuse in Boston and elsewhere attracted the attention of the Vatican. The Pope called an emergency summit for Cardinals regarding the crisis in the American Church. In a marked departure from the Church's backstage processing of such allegations, he called the sexual abuse of minors not only an "appalling sin," but also a "crime" (Investigative Staff 2002, p. 5), solidifying the shift into the domain of criminal justice authorities, and ending the implicit assumption that the Church should police "its own" through prayer or treatment, or both. Over the next few months, hundreds of victims in Boston came forward alleging abuse by dozens of priests. Nearly every turn in the litigation process was covered by the local news media, with much of it carried nationally.

As the accusations and the documentation multiplied, the Catholic laity began to respond. Churches across the Boston area and beyond held "listening sessions" for individuals to come together to vent anger and express confusion over the maelstrom of allegations (Wilgoren 2002). For the first time, masses of congregants questioned the way Church officials responded to incidents of abuse—usually by transferring the offending priest to another parish—and questioned the bad apple theory that had allowed the issue of clergy sexual abuse to lie relatively dormant. In this period of upheaval, a lay group called "Voice of the Faithful" (VOTF) sprang up and began to thrive (Muller and Kenney 2004).

The group's mission was tri-fold: to support the victims of abuse in their healing, to support priests of integrity, and to establish substantive change within the Church so the laity might have a meaningful voice in the Church structure (Muller and Kenney 2004). Unlike earlier dissenting groups, VOTF took a decidedly nonpolitical centrist stance, purposefully avoiding divisive issues like the role of homosexuals within the Church or priestly celibacy. Perhaps as a result of this moderate posture, the group burgeoned; four months after its inception, VOTF held a conference at the Hynes Convention Center in Boston, which attracted nearly 4,200 attendees (Muller and Kenney 2004). Within eighteen months, more than 200 chapters had been incorporated worldwide. Indeed, the popularity of VOTF proved that the natives were not only restless, but also that they were online and connected to one another, a combination that proved explosive for the Church. Through the internet, a story in Boston could be—and was—publicized across the world instantaneously and with vivid imagery. Rallies and protests outside the Boston Archdiocese were well chronicled. Messages proclaiming "Shame," "Pimp," and "Honk if you want Cardinal Law to resign" were sent across oceans, linking the international Catholic community to share in the disgrace, disillusionment, and anger that the Boston scandal had opened.

Somewhat ironically, VOTF's voice of dissent was fueled in great part by Catholic doctrine. Some readings of Vatican II documents, particularly those in *Lumen Gentium,* provided the laity with a mandate that allowed them—some would say required them—to vocalize discontent with the Church. That discontent was then broadcast around the world. VOTF's popularity was a key piece in the Catholic Church's scandal of 2002, because for perhaps the first time in recent history the laity—left, right, and center—were united in their condemnation of the hierarchy's behavior in its response to abuse. There was widespread agreement that the Church could not go on without some changes (Gibson 2003).

Over the next few months, both media coverage and litigation against the Archdiocese exploded. By June 2002—less than six months after publication of the *Globe* investigative report—more than 12,000 stories about priests abusing children had appeared in the major news media outlets (Steinfels 2003). Stories about the Catholic Church and its complicity were ubiquitous. Before the year's end, more than 550 people had filed suit against the Archdiocese over sexual abuse perpetrated by priests or other personnel[6], marking unprecedented action against any Archdiocese. The litigation then brought about an unparalleled pressure and query for more classified documents, which were also made public in an unusually high-profile fashion. Perhaps one of the most distinctive attributes of this litigation was its public nature and growing support by Catholics. Previously, such lawsuits were hushed and support for civil action was limited. With the litigation explosion in 2002, victims had the attention of the media and lay Catholics rallied to their defense.

Under Cardinal Law's direction, litigation strategies were adversarial, marked more by legal maneuvering than pastoral outreach and the Church seemed leery to accept responsibility publicly for sexual abuse in the priesthood. Law acknowledged that he had reassigned abusing priests, but blamed the problem on poor record keeping (McNamara 2002). During this time, the Archdiocese attempted to subpoena records from a therapist at its own Office of Healing, instituted only a few months earlier to assist victims of abuse (Ranalli 2003). In that same month, the Archdiocese filed papers alleging that responsibility for one victim's abuse lay with the victim himself and his parents' negligence (McNamara 2003)[7]. Although such a filing was dubbed as fairly standard in such cases, most viewed it as a hardball litigation tactic, and at the very least, unacceptable for a religious institution.

Later in the year, after settling with 86 survivors of John Geoghan for $10 million in September, the Archdiocese publicly acknowledged that it was contemplating filing for bankruptcy (Robinson and Kurkjian 2002). Considering the extensive wealth of the Archdiocese, the plea struck many as hollow: another move of gamesmanship in an adversarial process designed to shield the Church's wealth, to engender sympathy for the Church, and to stir resentment toward the victims. Cardinal Law eventually abandoned this idea, but many saw it as a ploy to drum up sympathy for the litigation-beleaguered Church in order to protect the Church's assets.

In December 2002, another set of documents was released that chronicled Cardinal Law's knowledge and warnings about several pedophilic priests (Farragher 2002), making it nearly impossible for him to continue to lead the Archdiocese. Although he had stated in early 2002, "When there are problems in the family, you don't walk away," many felt that his insistence on remaining in his post obstructed healing within the community. Lay groups, even Voice of the Faithful—which had deliberately tried to remain nonpolitical up to that point—eventually requested Law's resignation. Donations to the Church had dwindled. Law stepped down from his post in December 2002 and Bishop Richard Lennon was named Interim Head of the Archdiocese. During Lennon's term, litigation negotiations accelerated but a settlement was not reached.

In July 2003, Bishop Sean O'Malley, a Capuchin priest experienced in managing dioceses embroiled in clergy sexual abuse litigation, took over as head of the Boston Archdiocese[8]. In both public and private conversations, O'Malley expressed his desire to bring closure to the litigation, and he swiftly appointed new counsel to facilitate negotiations. Within two months, a tentative agreement was reached. An unprecedented $85 million was offered to victims on the condition that at least 80 percent of the victims signed on. Generally, victims were offered between $80 and $300 thousand, depending upon the extent of the abuse and related damages. The quota was quickly met, and a whirlwind of arbitration occurred during November and December 2003. Despite the extensive media coverage of the settlement negotiations, the arbitrations occurred with little fanfare or media exposure. The resolution of the previous two years of crisis occurred quietly. The process of rebuilding would be another story.

The John Jay Report and Forward

Shortly after the Boston Global Settlement, the *John Jay Report*, commissioned by the United States Conference of Catholic Bishops (USCCB), was released. This report was significant because it represented the first public acknowledgement of the problem of clergy sexual abuse by the Catholic Church in the U.S., and because it chronicled fifty years of official records on incidents of abuse. The problem was plainly stated as a matter of fact, and the study provided the evidence to support that assertion. This was nothing short of a breakthrough. The findings of this report, although limited because the source of the data came directly through dioceses reporting, are worth noting because they are an official record accepted by the Church.

The *John Jay Report* indicated that clergy sexual abuse within the Catholic Church was indeed widespread. It included a survey of 195 dioceses, eparchies[9], and other religious communities in the United States. 95 percent reported at least one allegation against a priest between 1950 and 2002. The report cited more than 4,000 incidents of abuse involving nearly 11,000 priests and deacons, who represented between 3 and 6 percent of the priestly population. Nearly 75 percent of the reported incidents occurred between 1960 and 1984, trailing off significantly after that point. The 2003 study also confirmed that reported abuse was disproportionately perpetrated against boys; 81 percent of the victims were male[10], and a substantial proportion of victims could be classified as ephebophilic (involving adolescent boys)[11], rather than pedophilic.

As noted, while the findings of the *John Jay Report* are both historical and enlightening, the study has significant limitations. First, researchers did not review the files themselves; instead they relied on self-reports from each diocese or religious community, which were not subject to any outside verification or review. Second, excluded from the report were cases in which the accuser was exonerated or the claim was retracted, a methodological decision which in most other circumstances might seem reasonable. However, in light of indications from reputable sources that many clergy abuse victims were bullied or intimidated into rescinding allegations, it is likely that these exclusions indicate a substantial undercount. Finally, those allegations chronicled in the *John Jay Report* can only be considered the tip of the iceberg in relation to the total number of incidents perpetrated during that fifty-year period. The same disincentives to official reporting of other types of crime apply here (e.g., belief that nothing will be done about it, viewing it as a private matter, fear of retaliation by the offender). In addition, the highly taboo nature of clergy sex crimes against children constitutes an additional disincentive.

While the Church accepted the findings of the report, they highlighted the fact that the lion's share of allegations occurred between the late sixties and the early eighties. In March 2004, a *New York Times* front-page headline read, "Abuse Scandal is Now 'History,' Top Bishop Says." Citing the downward trend in accusations and the new policies implemented by many dioceses across the country, Bishop Wilton Gregory claimed the Church had effectively "turned the page" in history. Although the accounting is accurate—and estimates over the last six years have reinforced the idea that the incidence of offending is indeed declining—any attempts to hurriedly move on appalled many victims and others touched by the scandal. Bishop Gregory's response, however, was hardly atypical; in the six years since this time, members of the Church have tried, repeatedly, many similar strategies to change the tenor of public discussion around the scandal. A variety of approaches have been attempted: claiming it was a problem of the past, blaming a salacious and unforgiving American media (Simpson 2010; Steinfels, 2003: p. 63), or even blaming the permissive culture of sexuality in America.

Although there have been worldwide reports about clergy sexual abuse within the Catholic Church since the Boston settlement, within the Vatican the problem had been dubbed by some as a uniquely American problem. However, in the wake of the Irish report, which chronicled the decades-long sexual and physical abuse in Irish orphanages, this assertion became less and less defensible. This inquiry catalogued the endemic abuse, involving extensive rape and molestation of thousands of children (McDonald 2009), and it marked another international watershed in clergy sexual abuse within the Catholic Church.

In response to some of the containment strategies which the Church has pushed, several now entrenched dissent groups, including Survivors Network of those Abused by Priests (SNAP), Irish Survivors of Child Abuse (ISOCA), BishopAccountability.org, and Voice of the Faithful (VOTF) have continually tried to reframe the issue, in particular to shift blame to the bishops involved in covering up for the sexual offenders. These groups have kept disgruntled Catholics, as well as those no longer affiliated with the religion, connected in many ways. Interest in these groups has ebbed and flowed over the years, but their persistence—and international appeal—speaks to the continued discontent with the Church over this issue.

Between 2004 and 2010, litigation sprung up in dozens of dioceses across the world in similar style as the Boston litigation: individual litigants coalesce into mass litigation, individual diocese and archdiocese were held liable for engaging in geographic solutions of sexually abusive priests, settlements often involved the release of previously sealed Church documents, and the suits were usually punctuated by multi-million dollar awards. Until 2010, this model had become the norm. Most recently, however, a new wave of litigation has been initiated, which attempts to engage the highest corners of the Church. Lawsuits in Kentucky, Wisconsin, and Oregon have recently named the Holy See as a liable party in cases where bishops failed to respond to credible allegations of sexual abuse, citing that the bishops were essentially subordinates following orders (Winfield 2010a). The

Vatican's legal response has been to assert that bishops are not Vatican employees, and therefore, it cannot be held liable in lawsuits (Winfield 2010b). Considering that bishops are appointed to their positions by the Pope and swear allegiance to him—not to mention mountains of Catholic dogma that dictates the Pope's encyclicals be obediently followed—this recent legal filing strikes many as chicanery on the Church's part.

It is yet to be determined whether this new legal strategy, however, will be successful for plaintiffs. Although the Kentucky lawsuits were dropped in August 2010—with the plaintiffs' attorney claiming the U.S. courts had imposed an "impossible burden" on his clients (Jones 2010)—the Supreme Court declined to dismiss the Oregon lawsuit, in essence giving a green light to plaintiffs on the issue of Papal immunity (Catholic News Agency 2010).

Moreover, credible allegations asserting Pope Benedict XVI was involved in the scandal have been circulated in the mainstream media. In the discovery process from this new wave of litigation, questions have arisen about Pope Benedict's involvement in concealing information about abusive priests in both Germany and America in the 1990s in his capacity as Cardinal. Newly public documents obtained by the Associated Press chronicled how Ratzinger effectively stalled the laicization (i.e., defrocking) of a pedophile priest, Stephen Kiesle in California, accused of tying up two children and violently abusing them. Kiesle was later convicted of the crimes. However, at the time, Ratzinger warned the corresponding bishop in writing that if such accusations were made public, they could harm, "the good of the universal Church" (Goodstein and Luo 2010).

In summary, since the Boston litigation, the Catholic Church sexual abuse crisis has played out in many ways. Numerous grand juries have been convened to investigate potential criminal charges (Associated Press 2003)[12]; more litigation has been initiated and settled; thousands of pages of previously sealed documents have been brought out into the light of day; investigative inquiries have been undertaken; bishops in Norway, Ireland, Belgium, Germany, and America have resigned under a cloud of scandal (Latza Nadeau 2010); and hundreds of millions of dollars have been spent in settlement and expenses. It is no wonder then, that in April 2010, Pope Benedict XVI stated that the crisis was "truly terrifying" (Latza Nadeau 2010).

Theoretical Foundations

As noted earlier in this chapter, clergy sexual abuse is a complex phenomenon, and my inquiry into the topic required some guidance from several different theoretical perspectives, including victimology, psychology, and justice studies. This research examines clergy sexual abuse litigation: why the survivors chose civil litigation, what they hoped to get out of it, and whether they felt they achieved justice. These questions traverse multiple disciplinary boundaries, but at their foundation, they are questions about law in our society, and specifically, the process by which a personal injury is transformed into a formal legal dispute. Felstiner, Abel, and Sarat provide an essential framework for understanding this dynamic and sometimes volatile process (1980-1981). They posit that disputes take shape as the meaning of harm to victims evolves from the identification of an experience as injurious (naming), to identifying a party/parties at fault (blaming), to the making of a claim (claiming), and, eventually, to litigation or some other method of formal resolution (disputing). The process by which personal injuries result in litigation or are "lumped" (i.e., endured without formal redress) is largely subjective, occurring in the personal as well as the social realms (Goffman 1963).

Theorists have offered two primary perspectives to explain why people initiate litigation. Resource mobilization theory (Cornell 1990; Galanter 1974) postulates that people pursue litigation based on a rational calculus: an aggrieved party, perhaps in consultation with others, takes an inventory of the time, money, and resources that would be involved in initiating civil proceedings, then balances these potential costs against how much he or she perceives could be won through such proceedings. This theory helps to explain why people of financial means are overrepresented in the tort system—as one attorney aptly put it, "It takes a lot of money to make a lot of money" (Morgan 1999)—and why people with few resources less frequently initiate lawsuits, even though their financial need may be greater than that of other potential litigants. Harr's account of the Woburn cancer cluster cases against the corporate giants Beatrice Foods and W.R. Grace provides a vivid example of the intimidation that potential litigants face if they are unfamiliar with the vicissitudes of litigation:

> Everything Richard Aufiero [the plaintiff] knew about lawyers he'd learned from television and the movies … He was scheduled to go into Boston on the morning of January 7, 1985, to have his deposition taken by the lawyers for W. R. Grace and Beatrice Foods. He awoke early that morning, feeling nervous. He imagined that the lawyers for

the big companies would badger him, try to trick him into saying damaging things, or make him look stupid (Harr 1995, p. 149).

To Richard, the room seemed crowded with lawyers. He counted eight of them, all wearing dark suits, and sitting around a long rectangular table. Their conversation stopped as he entered the room and he felt their gazes turn on him—cool, appraising stares (Harr 1995, p. 151).

The image of savvy lawyers arranged around a conference table staring down the blue collar man is stark, and is illustrative of Gallanter's theory of why the financially and socially disadvantaged shy away from litigation.

Gallanter does suggest that in some cases the "have nots" are able to come forward as a result of "strategic positioning." By pooling their claims, "one-shotters," who are strategically disadvantaged because of their lack of knowledge about the litigation process, are given more of a platform to battle "repeat players" who are generally savvier. He suggests that there is power in numbers: bringing together many "one-shotters" creates a more even dynamic, leveling the playing field. This dynamic was evident in the sexual assault cases lodged against Wall Street giants Merrill Lynch and Smith Barney:

This was a story that literally had legs. ... None of the firms anticipated the domino effect that took over as women heard about the plights of others similarly situated and grew bolder. To anyone who appreciated how threatening a giant brokerage firm could look to an employee, the confidence that had built among women with stories to tell was remarkable. Those who had suffered in silence, or striven to be one of the boys, were talking—first among themselves and now to the media (Antilla, 2003, pp. 197-198).

This dynamic could also explain why so many victims came forward after the *Globe* Spotlight series appeared in January 2002. In these cases, the plaintiffs' bar had become highly specialized, with several attorneys acting as "repeat players" against the Church. Because of this, the individual plaintiffs—who would otherwise have been the prototypical "one-shotters"—became instantly connected to powerful legal resources, providing an important impetus for individual survivors to sue.

Still, the implicit assumption in resource mobilization theory is that the primary goal of litigation is pecuniary gain: plaintiffs stand to make money, whether it be recouping expenses of lost work, lost health, lost profits, or other expenses (Morgan 1999), or through punitive awards that serve to punish the opposing party. Mather and Yngvesson (1980-

1981) note that tort actions typically focus disputes from something very complex into the simple language of money:

> ... a personal injury plaintiff describes an accident to his lawyer in terms of a broad range of medical, emotional, family, work-related and other concerns; the lawyer then rephrases the account in terms of a dollars and cents description of the case. Translation into the terms of a currency, such as money ... converts the complex into the straightforward; significantly, however, it also reinforces the dominance of a particular currency as the standard through which people, products, and other resources are made commensurable (p. 784).

Luban (1995, p. 2646) calls this process "the monetization of litigation." Typically, wins or losses are assessed through the symbolic language of money: the higher the award, the greater the victory.

Resource mobilization theory has received some empirical support. In their study of adverse birth outcomes, Sloan and Hsieh (1995) found that injury victims who faced comparatively low costs for making a claim were more likely to sue than those whose costs were higher. However, claims were also less likely to occur when victims' families had health insurance. This cost-benefit analysis did not occur in a vacuum: Sloan and Hsieh note that those cases in which an independent evaluator noted negligence were also more likely to proceed with formal claims (1995), suggesting that more substantively injurious experiences are more likely to result in litigation. Similarly, Miethe's (1995) study of litigiousness suggests that those with greater financial and legal resources are more likely to sue. Resource mobilization theory, however, does not explain why "have nots" choose to litigate, particularly why someone would be motivated to litigate when perceived personal costs are likely to weigh much more heavily in the balance against financial incentives.

In the case of clergy sexual abuse, disincentives to litigation are many and substantial. Clergy sexual abuse involves a constellation of taboos, or "discreditable information" (Goffman 1963), that many survivors do not want others to know. For instance, male victims frequently believe that knowledge of their sexual victimization will make them appear weak and vulnerable (Lew 1990). Further, because of stereotypes that male sexual abuse victims are likely to become sexual predators, victims also fear that significant relationships will be threatened if people learn of their victimization. Similarly, stereotypes that female sexual abuse victims become promiscuous generate fear of exposure among female victims. Beyond the stigma and disruption associated with the application of these stereotypes, plaintiffs also fear that they will be criticized as opportunistic and money hungry, a tack that the Church has used in the past to intimidate survivors (Frawley-O'Dea 2004, p. 14). Capturing the reality of this sentiment, Kennedy (1993, p. 8) writes, "Those who seek redress from the church as an institution are necessarily perceived as enemies trying to scale its walls and plunder its treasury."

Relational theorists, alternatively, assert the centrality of relationships in the decision to sue (Morgan 1999). In her study of litigation decision-making among sexually harassed women, Morgan notes that maternal responsibilities and marital commitment weighed most heavily for women contemplating civil action against their employers (1999). This influence was bi-directional: if families or spouses supported the litigation, the victim was more likely to sue; if they did not, they were more likely to avoid litigation or any further action. Women who decided to sue generally had "love as a litigation asset": they anticipated that support from friends and family would cushion the "insults of litigation," such as having their motives and truthfulness questioned, and having to endure extensive processing delays (Morgan 1999). Social support networks were viewed as critical to handling such adversity.

Included in the relational theorists' perspective is the attorney-client relationship. In his study of litigiousness, Miethe (1995) found that persons who had prior experience with legal disputes, those who had more positive attitudes about attorneys, and those who held more favorable views of the power of legal institutions to resolve conflict were more amenable to litigating. In this way, development of a positive relationship with an attorney may be a source of encouragement and support that serves as a buffer against personal assaults from outsiders.

But more than assessing the personal and social costs of the process of litigation, relational theorists also highlight different goals of litigation than other theorists. Rather than view litigation as a means to some financial end, relational theorists suggest that litigation presents an opportunity to negotiate one's personal and social identity. While one often hears stories of plaintiffs "hitting the jackpot" or finding "deep pockets," many theorists have suggested that the meaning of litigation transcends pecuniary gain to more personal or lofty justice goals. These include finding voice or autonomy, building social capital, seeking apologies, establishing history, and exploding the cause from select individuals to the larger community.

Finding Voice/Autonomy

Other studies note the importance of personal justice goals in justice. In particular, finding voice through litigation or using litigation as an expression of autonomy have been cited in several studies (Morgan 1999; Bumiller 1988; McCann 1994; May and Stengel 1990). Each suggests that the meaning of litigation runs much deeper than financial gain, and that principles of self-worth and autonomy may lie at the heart of pursuing civil claims.

These goals may involve using litigation as a vehicle to give the victim a voice. In Morgan's (1999) study of women who had been sexually harassed, she cites three women who used litigation as a way to establish their own personal independence. Ackerman (2002) echoes this sentiment, and adds that not only is voice important, but also so is vindication:

> When we employ a dispute resolution process, such as litigation, we use it in part to obtain a concrete result, such as financial compensation. But we also invoke the process (and this may be more true of public than private processes) to obtain the community's blessing on our cause: a recognition of its justice, a ratification of our course of action, a vindication, be it public or private. Even when private processes, such as mediation and arbitration, are employed, parties are likely to emerge most satisfied when they have been given "voice" (i.e., when they have been sufficiently heard), and when they have been treated as fully enfranchised members of the community (p. 6).

Particularly in cases where the injurious event is especially demeaning or demoralizing (e.g., sexual harassment or sexual abuse), the litigant may desire to regain some power over the perpetrator.

Implicit in any discussion about voice are notions of relational control. Goffman (1959) refers to this as defining the roles of social interaction, and in the case of litigation, the roles of social interaction are set in a consequential, dramatic framework which enables the previously powerless to begin to make demands. Goffman also notes the "distinctive moral character" involved in such redefinition. Win or lose, the opposing party is put in a position where it has to defend itself and its actions. Also, the compulsory legal process often involves acquiring information that can be made public, serving to raise awareness about a particular topic. In theory, Goffman would predict that this process should be empowering for victims. In practice, however, the realities of court delays, complicated legal maneuvering, and the limitations of a civil court to force acceptance of moral responsibility may frustrate victims (O'Brien 1992). How important the platform and the redefinition of roles were in clergy sexual abuse litigation remains an open question.

Building Social Capital

Gallanter hints at the idea of litigation as a means of building social capital when he speaks of class action as "strategic positioning" for the "have nots," although he references this positioning mostly insofar as it provides a platform from which litigants can pursue the goal of pecuniary gain. This framing misses the potential centrality of community building suggested by Ackerman (2002), who opines:

> We search for community in the course of conflict not so much because it is imposed upon us or because of some artificial dictate. In a free country, community doesn't seek us. Community is what we seek ... We sue because we feel that we have been wronged, that our world has been knocked out of balance, and we wish to restore a sense of harmony to our lives and our relationships with those who surround us (p. 6).

In this sense, the implications of litigation transcend traditional pecuniary gains and move into the realm of building connections within the community.

Specifically, the goal of building two types of social capital may be promoted within the group of victims and within the larger community. Putnam (2000) refers to these as "bonding" and "bridging." "Bonding" social capital involves connecting with others within your immediate community; it is an inward looking process that "cements homogeneous groups" (Ackerman 2002), while "bridging" involves looking outward and connecting diverse people together.

When asked about the priorities of the Agent Orange class action litigation, the veteran who had coordinated the litigation stated, "We want to turn the American people around so that the Vietnam combat soldier will no longer be abused and dishonored" (1987, p. 44). Such anecdotal information supports the theory that bridging one community to a larger community could be a driving force in the transformation of disputes. In fact, the negative reception that veterans received after returning home proved to be a big motivator for many of the veterans. In the following quote from *Strangers at Home*, Figley and Levantam (as quoted in Schuck 1987) note the importance of both bonding and bridging social capital in the context of Agent Orange litigation through the drama of a combat soldier's reception upon his return home from Vietnam:

> Walking across the Boston Common his first day home, his service uniform and gear fully apparent, he was greeted by peace demonstrators with shouts of "Killer! How many babies did you burn over there?" Returning home, his brother offered, "You asshole! Why did you go to Vietnam anyway?" Seeking solace and companionship that night in the American Legion Hall, he was confronted with "Hey buddy! How come you guys lost the war over there?" (p. 25).

The litigation movement grew out of this context: Vietnam veterans wanted to reinstate their dignity as soldiers and defenders of freedom.

Restorative Goals: The Role of Apology

Several legal scholars have argued for a greater place for apology in the legal process (Latif 2001). Levi (1997) states: "Apologies ... alleviate tensions that lie at the core of public disputes and eliminate the fiction of translating emotional pain to dollars" (p. 1166). She asserts that some apologies have the power to address a power imbalance between the parties. This occurs when the offender acknowledges his or her "diminutive moral stature," and by so doing, affirms the importance of moral actions in general (Levi 1997). Minow (1998) also discusses the importance of community in true apologies:

> The mystery of apology depends upon the social relationship it summons and strengthens; the apology is not merely words. Crucial here is the communal nature of the process of apologizing. An apology is not a soliloquy. Instead, an apology requires communication between a wrongdoer and a victim; no apology occurs without the involvement of each party. Moreover, the methods for offering and accepting an apology both reflect and help to constitute a moral community. The apology reminds the wrongdoer of community norms because the apology admits to violating them (p. 114).

She adds that true apologies involve a "full acceptance of responsibility" (p. 115).

Restorative justice scholars argue that apologies need to be forward, rather than backward, focused in that the apology should focus on accepting responsibility so that the harm can be avoided in the future (Braithwaite 1994). Similarly, Brown (2004) acknowledges the need for the apology to also include the wrongdoer's affirmation of the validity of the rule that he or she broke.

Of course, apologies run the risk of being insincere or of being used manipulatively by the wrongdoer to avoid changing certain behaviors (Minow 1998). Latif (2001) notes that apologies that are coerced, partial, or safe (i.e., those which involve exceptions to rules of evidence) will lack some of the power for restoration that a "naked" apology would otherwise have.

Establishing History

Less frequently explored goals of litigation involve information gathering and establishing the truth. The Woburn class action suits illustrate both of these objectives. One victim states, "We're not in it for the money. We're in it to show that we've been harmed by what they did" (Harr 1995, p. 150). Another litigant echoes this sentiment:

> They're guilty of polluting. My child died from their stupidity. I didn't get into this for the money. I got into this because I want to find them guilty[13] for what they did. I want the world to know that (p. 442).

Another victim notes that the lawsuit was the only way to get information about what happened when they had been shut down by large corporations and the town. In the Agent Orange class action, the veteran who coordinated the efforts bluntly stated the following motivation for litigation: "We want to find out what is killing us" (Schuck 1987, p. 44).

This desire for information is not uncommon among plaintiffs. Legal scholar Wendy Wagner (2004) points out that, particularly in product liability or environmental law cases, agencies have a perverse incentive to conceal from the public information that may be damaging to their activities. She adds that because government regulation is so lax about agencies needing to provide information about the potential harms of their products, litigation can sometimes be the last resort vehicle to uncover such material. This goal of litigation—to establish the cause of some harm—was an important feature of litigation involving questions about the Bendectin, the Dalkon Shield, tobacco, Agent Orange, silicone breast implants, and tampons. In each of these cases, the plaintiffs were largely in the dark with respect to the capacity of the substance or device to induce health problems. Only through the compulsory process afforded by litigation was "stubborn information" uncovered (Wagner 2004).

Furthermore, because litigation has the potential to uncover abuses, it holds the power to provide a type of accounting for history. Legal scholar Martha Minow discusses the need to establish facts in the wake of human rights violations. Such was the logic of the Truth and Reconciliation Commission in South Africa—as well as others in Uruguay and Chile—: to come together to establish an accurate historical record. With this agreed upon testament, the community reconciles itself to its past—however sordid or horrific it might be. And because the society recognizes the harm in its past, it is more ready to move forward, so that it may not repeat the same mistakes. Litigation, however, is not typically thought of in terms of establishing truth.

Exploding the Cause: From Micro to Macro

Another potential reason for litigation involves transforming the dispute from micro to macro, a piece that Hagan (2002) notes is often forgotten when discussing motivations for litigation. Through litigation, the personal becomes both the public and the political. As Mather and Yngvesson (1981) note, by expanding the dispute victims have the potential to cause "social change" through "legal change." There are several notable cases that have pushed issues into national awareness: the Erin Brockovich case highlighted the hazards of pollutants and drinking water contaminants; the Woburn civil action cases drew attention to the correlation between toxins in the soil and leukemia clusters; the Thalidimide and Bendectin cases engendered awareness of the dangers of ingesting drugs during pregnancy; and the Wall Street cases underscored the psychological toll of sexual harassment in the workplace.

In many of these cases, the media was the agent for transforming the dispute from private to public. Lytton (2005, p. 82) argues that the media has framed the clergy sexual abuse litigation of 2002 in terms of rampant institutional abuse and the need for policy reform. These accounts have encouraged victims to use their traumatic experiences to prevent future abuses to others. It remains to be seen whether they will also bring about reform in the power structure of the Catholic Church.

In summary, there are varied theoretical approaches to understanding the pursuit of litigation and the impact of litigation on plaintiffs' lives. How these perspectives apply to the specific context of clergy sexual abuse is an empirical question, and one that I explore here. Using ethnographic methods, I apply the transformation of disputes framework to explicate the dispute process from the survivors' perspectives. As we shall see, the findings reveal the minimal role played by the desire for monetary compensation in the decision to sue, as well as the complexity of personal and interpersonal motivations, and the potential of litigation to be personally and socially transformative.

---

[1] Doyle would later report that he anticipated that bishops would nevertheless "do the right thing." At a 2004 speaking engagement, Doyle sadly noted that his expectations could not have been more wrong.

[2] For a more complete discussion of these factors, see Benyei 1998; Briere 1992; Urquiza and Capra 1990; Dimmock 1988; Finkelhor 1990; Lew 1990; Mendel 1995; Olsen 1990; Sauzier 1989. In particular, male victims may experience gendered responses and symptomology, including experiencing excessive shame, questioning their own masculinity or sexuality, or resisting disclosure for fear that others will believe the victimization makes them prone to sexual predation. For a more detailed discussion on selection of audience, see Goffman 1963, as well as Mather and Ygnvesson 1985.

[3] The Council also put forth several other groundbreaking documents, including the Declaration on Religious Liberty, which insisted on every human being's freedom from coercion to practice religion, as well as the Declaration of the Relation of the Church to Non-Christian Religions, which opened dialogue between Catholics and other religions, in particular, condemning anti-Semitism as a fundamentally anti-Catholic sentiment (Perko 1989).

[4] Geoghan was later murdered in prison by a fellow inmate.

[5] In Massachusetts, Chapter 119 (51a) sets out the mandatory reporting laws for personnel working with children, but MA. Chapter 233 (20a) does allow for exceptions for clergy when communications occur in the confessional. However, this exception does not exclude priests from mandatory reporting in general. For communications that occur outside the confessional, they have an obligation to report it, as do other personnel working with children when they have reason to suspect abuse or neglect.

[6] Other personnel include other religious men or women affiliated with the Archdiocese, including directors of religious education or deacons.

[7] The legal term was "contributory negligence."

[8] He had previously led both the Fall River and Palm Beach dioceses.

[9] Eparchies are a Catholic Church jurisdiction, similar to a diocese, of Eastern Rite Catholics living in the United States.

[10] Some have attributed this to bias in reporting, making female victims invisible. *Globe* columnist Eileen McNamara questioned the lack of attention the Vatican has paid to girl victims through recent condemnations of gay priests (2005).

[11] The use of the term "ephebophile" is controversial. Isely (1997) notes that the term is used primarily by clinicians working with abusive priests in an attempt to distinguish them from those who abuse younger children. This term is not mentioned in the *Diagnostic and Statistical Manual of Mental Disorders* (1994). Although ephebophilia is not listed in *Webster's New Collegiate Dictionary*, "ephebe" is listed, defined as "a young man."

[12] The following is a partial list of dioceses which have been involved in clergy sexual abuse litigation: Spokane, Washington; Paterson and Newark, NJ; Bridgeport, CT; Covington, Kentucky; Boston, Worcester, and Springfield,

MA; Orange County, Santa Rosa, Sacramento, Oakland, and Los Angeles, CA; Pittsburg, PA; Portland, OR; Denver, CO; Rockville (Long Island), NY; Rockford, IL; and Cleveland, OH.

[13] The actual legal finding would be "responsible."

3
Introducing the Survivors

The data for this research were generated through in-depth face-to-face[1] interviews with thirty-five key players in clergy sexual abuse litigation. The final sample is comprised of twenty-two survivors and thirteen advocates. This includes litigants, attorneys representing several local and national law firms, social service providers who work closely with survivor-litigants and non-litigants, and members of the Church. A complete discussion of the methodology is discussed in Appendix A.

Background

All of the survivors in the study were Caucasian and predominantly of Irish descent (fifteen of twenty two), although there were a handful of survivors who were of Italian, Polish, or French heritage. The survivors ranged in age from their late twenties to late fifties and included fifteen men and seven women. Eleven survivors were part of the Boston Global Settlement, six had litigated prior to 2002, and three had participated in litigation after the Boston litigation began in 2002. Two of the women were not litigants, although one had won a settlement to pay retroactively for therapy without officially filing a lawsuit, but with the assistance of an attorney intervening on her behalf. Both of these women were very active in the survivor community, in support groups, and in advocacy groups that kept them in regular contact with other survivors.

Although there were some extremes in the socio-economic backgrounds of the survivors during their childhoods, most were middle or lower middle class. At one extreme, one survivor related that her single mother raised seven children while working a minimum wage job, and was unable to provide adequate food and clothing without outside assistance. Another survivor relayed a similar story: seven children growing up in a small apartment, sleeping on the couch, reliant upon the church for a turkey donated for Thanksgiving dinner. At the other extreme, another survivor came from a financially stable, affluent background, complete with a summer home and nanny. Most survivors in the study, however, were from working class families. All of the survivors, with one exception, were from two-parent, intact homes, usually first or second generation Americans. Notably, most came from homes with five or more children; only one survivor was an only child.

Legal Advocate Background

The legal advocates in this research came from a variety of backgrounds. Several of the attorneys came from large law firms, others from medium sized firms, still other who were from very small firms, each of the firms having varying resources for clients. All but one of the attorneys interviewed had at least ten years experience working with these types of cases. Some firms were local, others not.

The socio-economic and ethnic backgrounds of legal advocates were not discussed in any depth in this research. Of the thirteen advocates, nine were Catholic, one Protestant, and three Jewish.

The Abuse

Although there were no questions about the abuse in the research protocol, all but two of the survivors talked about it, either in graphic detail, or in vague terms designed to convey the type of experience it was.[2] The participants in this study reported myriad types of abuse: one male survivor relayed stories of how the offending priest was a mentor to him, using more manipulation than force to meticulously groom him for abuse in adolescence; a female survivor described abuse beginning in grade school that lasted for years, so painful that she repressed the memories for decades. Another male related mostly "psychological abuse" that eventually led to one aggressive encounter; while one female relayed that she believed she was the priest's girlfriend when he pursued a sexual relationship with her in fifth grade; another woman talked about a single incident at age nine when she was brutally raped by a priest she did not know; another man talked about a strong friendship and counseling relationship between him and the priest which led from inappropriate sexual contact to very violent encounters. Of the survivors, two had been sexually abused by more than one priest—although it should be noted that several survivors reported that they had been sexually abused by other individuals either within or outside their families. Of the twenty-two survivors, only four relayed an isolated incident of abuse; the rest had been abused on several occasions. Of the four isolated incidents, three were described as violent batteries. Overall, there is little homogeneity in the type of abuse these survivors incurred, the age of onset, or the level of force used.

Just as the *John Jay Report* suggests that the vast majority of abuse occurred in the fifties, sixties, and seventies, all but two of the survivors in this study incurred their abuse before 1980. The two youngest participants related abuse occurring in the early eighties and early nineties.

In terms of how the priests gained access to these survivors, just as much of the anecdotal research already suggests that the survivors knew the offending priests through a variety of church-related activities, including serving as altar boys, parochial school involvement, and/or through close familial ties. In contrast to earlier anecdotal reports, the findings from this research do not support the view that sexual abuse victims come from single-parent and/or highly dysfunctional families. Several of the participants relayed very strong positive ties to their families. Beth, Edward, Fred, Andrew, Howard, Connie, Isaac, Marilyn, and Francis portray their parents and/or other caretaker figures in a generally positive light.

Finally, it is important to note that many of these survivors noted that either a close relative or close friend had also reported being abused by a priest in the past. In a few cases, they reported that this person had committed suicide or overdosed, in part a result from the abuse.

Pay, Pray, and Obey

Being a Roman Catholic in Boston means being part of a very distinct culture, one that reaches beyond the pew or the statehouse to the dinner table and the hearth, what writer David Gibson (2003) dubs, "a mix of tradition, ethnicity, and tribal loyalty" (p. 86). Sociologist Andrew Greeley observes that there is a unique "Catholic imagination" (as quoted by Groome 2002), a particular lens through which one views the world. Similarly, Groome reports that,

> ... [L]eaving a church is easy compared to erasing the traces of Catholic socialization. It has likely shaped their personhood and ways in the world, their defining images and stories, their values, virtues, and vices, their hopes and fears, even their sense of humor" (2002, p. XIII).

The survivors I spoke with relayed with vivid imagery the flavor of what it meant to be Catholic, particularly in their childhood. They painted a picture of a culture that afforded uncritical deference to its priests, unswerving attention to Catholic doctrine, and implicit faith in the universality and benevolence of the Church—as one survivor put, it was the "centerpiece" in his family's life.

Despite the differences in the type of abuse experiences that survivors relayed, there was remarkable consistency in the role of the Church in these survivors' lives. Although participation in church activities varied slightly by family, in general, all of the survivors as children attended weekly Mass and on Holy Days, and had some involvement beyond this in church life (e.g., being an altar boy, attending parochial school, or volunteering). Not surprisingly, survivors usually learned what it meant to be Catholic from their immediate families. In fact, all but one of the survivors described at least one parent as being "devout" (i.e., attending daily Mass, praying the rosary regularly, etc.). Henry relates his upbringing in the Catholic faith: "... I'm culturally a Catholic. I'm an Irish Catholic and there are no buts about that!" He goes on to say: "It was important to me. It was my life." The power of the requirement of obedience cannot be underestimated when considering clergy sexual abuse. Norman, a survivor and advocate, talked about the deference that not only he, but also his parents were supposed to afford the priest. "We learn other people matter more than we do." He referred to the very clear hierarchy of status and line of authority: parent over child, priest over parent, bishop over priest. He relayed an account when his priest-offender, prior to the onset of abuse, put him into a scissors-hold in the middle of the family living room, in front of his parents. The priest tickled him forcefully— which for this survivor was a dreaded activity. His parents watched in horror as, with his eyes, he silently pleaded for help, but they knew better than to say a word. In hindsight, Norman believed the incident— and his parents' inability to respond—sent an unmistakable message to his offender that inappropriate behavior would be overlooked. They dared not question the priest, however wildly inappropriate his behavior might have been. In a similar vein, Virginia's abuser had her give him backrubs in front of her parents when he would come over to visit. The parents simply did not question the behavior or intervene.

Matthew, another survivor, talks about the priest's role in the community:

> ... this guy was considered a saint. Next to saint. Everyone thought he was the best thing since sliced bread. Plus, during that time, 1977, priests were next to God. Their word came from God. You couldn't question them.

Lawrence expands on the role of the priest:

> You know, we were taught to look at the priests with a great deal of reverence and respect. That sort of reverence was accentuated in myself as a child because I was aware that the priest had sort of supernatural powers, could supposedly perform miracles on the altar, turn the wine into blood, turn the host into the body of Christ ... They could forgive sins. They could determine who was going to heaven and who was going to hell. You had to be in tight with the priest in order to get forgiven! [laughs] So they were like God's representative on earth is the way that the child views the priest. And that viewpoint was certainly supported by my parents.

Howard, whose family had donated heavily to the local church, talked about how another priest would not intercede on his behalf when he overheard an abusive priest throwing Howard violently around in the next room. The message was clear in these survivors' minds: the priests' lives mattered more than those of parishioners. The Catholic laity were to give of their time and money uncritically, while the priests set the rules of engagement.

The Catholic way of life went well beyond attending Mass or church-sponsored activities. Being Catholic meant being part of a community, and being part of that community carried responsibilities. For example, Howard talked of attending funerals in the community for anyone in the church with whom his family was even distantly familiar as part of the Catholic civic responsibility that had been instilled in him.

One indicator of the reach of the Church in the lives of survivors and their families was the frequent presence of priests in the home. Several of the survivors described frequent in-home contact with both the offender and other priests. Virginia describes how her family became close friends with her abuser, allowing him to come over and expecting her to prepare drinks (i.e., scotch whiskey) for him. Similarly, Greta remembers having one priest at her house for dinner regularly. George and Connie, respectively, capture the ubiquity of Catholicism in their lives:

> My family at that time was a typical family where the priests were friends of the family. There were priests coming in and out of our house, having dinner at our house and saying Mass at our house. Because of my parents' strong Catholic beliefs, the priests were part of the family.

> Priests and nuns were at our house all the time. My parents volunteered a lot for the Church. My dad was [worked for the

parochial school[3]]. Our family was entrenched in it ... So we just had constant [interaction] ... My parents' best friends were the nuns. They were just a big part of our lives. We were at church all the time.

Indeed, the survivors I spoke with had a great deal in common regarding this upbringing; still, whether these families are typical—as George suggested—in their Catholic upbringing is not clear. What is clear, however, is that being Catholic for these survivors was as much about social ties as it was about theology.

Further, being Catholic affected home life in a number of other ways. Matthew reports:

... it's hard to quantify ... Church was used as a weapon. Like, if I spilled the milk, I was going to hell, stuff like that. We had to go to church. There wasn't any question about it. Not daily Mass, but we did follow stuff on Lent, no meat on Fridays and whatever else ...

Finally, being Catholic meant protecting the Church against anyone or anything. Lewis relates his mother's insistence that he not go public with his accusations against the offending priest or she would disown him because the bishop had stated she would not be a "good Catholic" if her son filed a lawsuit. Fred relayed how he believed his mother was still emotionally tormented about having to say any untoward word about the Church, however true it was. Christopher described how after his disclosure, his family resorted to praying quietly for him, rather than support him in his activism to get the truth from the Church. This tendency—to protect the Church against even the truth—was ingrained in many of the survivors, and especially in their parents.

For survivors in this study, this culture of "pay, pray, and obey" was deeply ingrained. One survivor, Douglas, analogized being Catholic to being American: one is so submerged in the culture that it's almost impossible to detect its influence or to get away from its effect: "If I moved to France it wouldn't make me any less American. It's woven into the fiber of who I am." The legal advocates who had been raised Catholic relayed the same sentiment. Lynne stated: "I'll never not be Catholic. I toyed with the idea of other religions and it doesn't fit with what I was raised with ..." Similarly, several survivors referred to themselves as "recovering Catholics" in the same way that an alcoholic believes that he is never cured of his or her affliction. For these survivors, being Catholic was something they needed to get over in order to lead healthier lives.

The Lives They've Led

Both survivors and legal advocates observed that the survivor community is a diverse, sometimes fractious group. The following discussion addresses some of the socio-cultural differences within the group for the purpose of understanding the backgrounds that help shape survivors' interpretive processes.

Demographically, survivors' educational backgrounds varied widely: three had advanced degrees, while one had not finished high school. Some survivors were highly functioning in that they maintained lucrative businesses; others had poor or spotty employment histories. These differences in demography shape the meanings different survivors assigned to their experiences. Beth describes the complexity within the survivor community:

> I remember [another survivor] saying, "They think that we all live in some orphanage somewhere." The vision of the poor victim who is addicted to drugs and can't keep a job ... most of us are not that. And we may have gotten close to some of that. We all know what it's like to think about suicide here and there, but many, many, many of us have been successful in the eyes of the world. We aren't only our abuse. I mean, yeah, it has affected us.

Still, as Beth mentioned, some threads were common to many of the survivors. Not surprisingly, almost everyone reported having a difficult adolescence, subsequent to the abuse. Often survivors saw the abuse as an experience that put them on a bad life trajectory—a "ditch" as one survivor put it—that frequently led to alcoholism or drug addiction. For example, Fred and Howard, respectively, describe similar breaks from the Church after the abuse:

> [A]fter this abuse I wanted nothing to do with the Church. I didn't know it was the abuse—I just was negative about the whole ... [trails off]. By the end of eighth grade I was *done*. I was done. And I never went back to Mass. I left home at fifteen. I was heavily into drug abuse and alcohol at fifteen.

> [After confirmation] I never looked back. And I never went back to Church after that. I started fucking off. I started getting in trouble. I started on drugs. I started getting high. I got caught in the seventh grade, I'm doing [pills]. I mean, I'm out of control ... I'm getting high. I'm smoking opium. I was fourteen years old!

Similarly, Greta and Rick, respectively, discuss drinking as a coping mechanism that sprang out of abuse too painful to deal with:

> I tried to get sober ... but ... I couldn't. I went to AA every day. It was a year here, six months, three weeks [sober]. I couldn't stop. It was always that something too painful happened. Emotionally, I couldn't deal with it, so I drank.

> All my broken relationships, my series of friends, deviated sex ... It was just deviant, insane stuff. And I would drink over it because I knew it wasn't healthy. And then I would do what I would do and then I would get drunk and take drugs to allow me to do it, and then I would do it and feel bad and drink and take drugs. It was a vicious circle ... all as a result of what happened as a child ...

Five survivors participated in a twelve-step program for their alcoholism, while a sixth underwent other alcohol-related therapy for addictions cultivated in adolescence as an escape from reality. However, not all of the survivors I spoke with had begun to deal with their addictions. Matthew talks about the role of alcohol in his life currently:

> I know one of the things of the 553 of us [Boston litigants] or however many of us there are, too, is that a common theme is drugs and alcoholism. The amount of alcohol that I consume would make most folks unconscious. That's why I drink that much, to eventually become unconscious. Because it gives me a few hours of relief at night, where I don't have nightmares, where I'm actually unconscious, and I don't have to feel. [pause] It's expensive.

Lewis, also still using, states that he "hasn't cut everything [cocaine and alcohol] completely out," but has things, "more under control."

Survivors' interpersonal relationships were also diverse. Jeff, who has had several failed relationships, tracks his relational dysfunction back to his abuse:

> Then it was actually [another survivor] who said, "So let me get this straight: every time you're involved with a woman, and then you talk about love, you're not interested. You never thought that that was because the first time you had sex it was with a man and he was a priest and you were an altar boy and you were eleven?" You know, I just never ... You have to laugh because the hindsight of it is that it's so blatantly obvious.

Isaac echoes the sentiment that the abuse shaped his inability to be part of a committed relationship:

I'm not married. I do not own a home. I do not have a full-time job. I do not have health insurance … I'm [in my forties].[4] Ok? I should be there already. Ok? I also have regrets about how this event seemed to lead me off in a ditch, if you will. Might I be different without it? Might I have a family, children of my own? Maybe.

Similarly, Greta talks about the abuse as being pivotal in her history of failed relationships. Still, not every survivor portrayed this type of instability in maintaining relationships. Three survivors had been married for two decades each, two for approximately ten years, and the youngest survivor had been married for a few years.

Job instability, frequent residential moves, and bouts of depression—sometimes involving suicidal ideation—also emerged as prominent themes among many survivors. Even those who had maintained successful careers reported erratic moving patterns. Virginia, like several other survivors, was successful in her career but much less stable in her private life:

I ran. I moved. I was in a variety of states in a variety of jobs … I married a guy who I'd met at a bar. He came to live with me a week after that. He was kind of homeless. And I just didn't want to be alone. And he'd get fired or quit and every six months to a year we'd move. I tried to … [trails off] My therapist one time wanted me to write down where I'd lived, and I couldn't even follow my W-2 forms and get every place. So I ran … I was never comfortable in my own skin.

Perhaps most interesting is that these categories of relationship dysfunction, poor employment history, and alcoholism/drug abuse were independent of each other. While Virginia was an alcoholic and reports a period in her life when moving was erratic, she always was able to support herself through a prestigious occupation. Similarly, Fred reports a constant battle with alcohol, but was always able to maintain his own business. Even Beth, who was in a stable relationship and had a solid career, stated that the abuse had taken its' toll, saying, "I'll never be a good sleeper … I'm always going to lead with my anxiety."

In terms of spirituality, the survivors relayed myriad responses. Several survivors relayed a sense of profound loss that they no longer believed in the religion:

If they intervened when I reported it, they could have saved me from losing my spirituality, which is completely gone. I was like, halfway down the road to being a priest and now I wake up in the middle of the night afraid of dying because now I think that that's it—it's all over. And I have panic attacks. And that's—they had their chance when I reported to stop it because it was only six months after the incident. They didn't do that. (Francis)

[Speaking about his daughter:] I feel enormously lax for not having given [her] any sense of spiritual practice. I feel like it is an enormous deficit in her life. And yet, I have no spiritual practice and have never been able to trust any kind of ... I can't trust God. And ... [breaks down crying] ... It feels terrible to me that she has no sense of God or any sense of spiritual practice and I don't know what to do about it. I feel like, at some point, in her adult life, she'll probably turn out to be a missionary somewhere! [laughs] [slowly, painfully:] But that to me is the biggest loss of it all, the sense of spiritual practice. (Henry)

Howard's response illustrates the ambiguity regarding his feelings about the Church and its teachings:

[Regarding spirituality:] I don't know what I am. [pause] I don't. I mean, I want to say it, but I can't. I learned all my morals in the Catholic Church. I am a Catholic. No doubt about it ... I learned all my values here ... I actually understand the symbolism of it. It reaches out to me. I can't. I mean, I can't stand what has happened ... And it sucks. Sucks. Because it's a great religion and you've got some assholes running it.

It is perhaps easy to understand why few held any remaining positive feelings about the Catholic Church, but this did not necessarily mean they felt no spirituality. One man practiced eastern transcendentalism, while others sensed God as a presence but did not subscribe to any particular religion. Still others felt God was very much a part of their lives, leading them in their fight against the Church.

---

[1] Three interviews were conducted by phone with legal advocates who were not local to Boston.

[2] When survivors began to get into more detail, I reminded them that they did not need to discuss the abuse, but that I would listen to whatever they thought was important. At this point, the survivors would usually state that talking relieved them of some shame, and that it was healthy for them.

[3] Any identifying information has also been filtered to protect the survivors' identities.

[4] His precise age has been changed to preserve confidentiality.

4

The Road to Litigation

Although Sherman (1993) initially conceived defiance theory to explain why people engage in criminal behavior, I would argue that the same components—social distance, legitimacy, shame, and pride—are relevant in understanding this litigation as an act of defiance against the Catholic Church. For survivors, litigation meant digging in their heels about the abuse they incurred, standing their ground, and ultimately, defying the institution that had shut its eyes to the abuse going on in its' sight. For most of these survivors, litigation was, in great part, a rejection of Church laws and rules, a formal movement from "insider" to "outsider" in the Church. This disobedience was usually an extension of the already established lesser disobediences of not attending Mass or participating in other Catholic rituals.

Early Points in the Transformation of the Experience

Most acts of defiance have precursors, and this litigation is no different. As Felstiner et al. (1981) note, before a dispute occurs, the experience must first be transformed through the "naming, blaming, and claiming" stages. With clergy sexual abuse litigation, the notion of defiance is pivotal in understanding how many survivors moved through this transformation, particularly in the stages of blaming and claiming. Sherman's recipe for defiance sheds light on how survivors distanced themselves from the institution (in this case, the Church), lost faith in its legitimacy, coped with disintegrative shame, and finally, began to feel emboldening pride in their journey to civil action. Although every survivor told a different and unique story, every survivor recognized these components, albeit in different fashions.

Social Bonds: Leaving Behind the Unholy Temple

Even though the respondents in this study had a variety of motivations for the litigation, and often had come from very different walks of life, the one consistent thread among all of them was that they were no longer practicing Catholics. With varying levels of volition, survivors generally each went through their own process of distancing themselves from the Church. Sometimes this involved a series of failed interactions or attempts at rectification; other times survivors simply drifted away as a consequence of the abuse. In either case, the social distance needed to be wide enough to justify the avenue of formal disputing: litigation.

The litigation was very much like a divorce for many survivors. They had all left the Church at some point, usually long before any thought of litigation occurred. This point of transformation is critical: Some had broken their bonds to the Church when the abuse happened, while for others, the social distance widened more slowly. Fred talks about his abrupt break from the Church, which had previously been an important part of his family:

> And I got scholarships that I ended up throwing away after this because I didn't want to go to parochial school ... I don't even think I told my parents. I threw them in a barrel ... Because after this abuse I wanted nothing to do with the Church.

Similarly, Douglas discusses his growing aversion for the Church and its hypocrisy

> By age 15, going to Mass—I would put my arms up on the pew and say, [sarcastically] "So what time does this show start?" And my mother was just eventually like, "You don't have to go to church."

His aversion for the Church grew to the point that he eventually approached a priest and demanded to be excommunicated, which the priest refused to do.

Francis describes his process of becoming un-tethered from the Church's moorings:

> A few months later [after the abuse] I started falling out of going to church. I was just about completely out within a year.

On some level, Douglas, Fred, Lewis, and Francis knew at the time of their victimizations that the incidents were abusive. Becoming disconnected from the Church was a byproduct of identifying the abuse (naming) and ascribing some level of blame (to someone or something).

Others, like Henry, Virginia, and Marilyn, spent more time in the "naming" stage, perhaps not fully understanding that the experience was abusive because the priest groomed them to believe he helped them by his actions. Because they initially didn't perceive the experience as injurious, their links to the Church were in less jeopardy during the time of the abuse. Once they realized the harm involved in the experience and were able to name it, the social distance between them, the Church, and their perpetrators widened.

On the other end of the spectrum, others talked about trying desperately to remain in the Church. Caught between the naming and blaming stages, Connie spoke emotionally about how she attended church regularly until she began to deal with the abuse in therapy:

> I tried to keep going! It was crazy because I would go—not during a Mass, but just sit there in the empty church. And I would just think … I used to find such solace. I really did. The Church was such a spiritual house for me, for all those years.

Her sense of disillusionment with the Church grew during her period of self revelation and eventually culminated in her filing an act of apostasy—an official motion to un-baptize oneself out of the faith. However, she continued to attend well into her adulthood, more than twenty years after she had been abused. At that point, the blaming process had morphed to include both the priest and the Church. The only person to continue to attend Mass regularly through the beginning of litigation was Edward, and his attendance dropped off precipitously when he perceived a lack of empathy from his parish community:

> My Church has not reached out to me. My kids went to parochial school. And now the only thing I get from them is form letters to get donations. They just don't seem to get it … It's business as usual.

Most of the survivors I spoke with, however, left the Church shortly after the abuse, usually during adolescence, with little fanfare or ceremony, subsequently attending church services for "weddings and funerals only." The commonality was an alienation from the Church as they came to understand it. Even the three survivors who had remained active in the Church into adulthood (i.e., Connie, Edward, and Isaac) came to understand that the Church of their childhood was not the Church they had come to know.

Hypocrisy/Legitimacy

Social distance, however, is a necessary but insufficient precursor for litigation; by itself it cannot explain how people turned to litigation. The coupling of social distance with a crisis of legitimacy, however, begins to explain why these survivors litigated. Perhaps one of the most important themes that survivors discussed was hypocrisy within the Church. Even though full awareness about the extent of the crisis was still not known prior to the public revelation of Church documents in 2002, survivors had begun to ascribe blame to the Church for other things; it was almost as if they sensed the Church's culpability. The seeds of defiance had already taken root prior to any civil action for nearly every survivor with whom I spoke. Indeed, some of the most emotional moments in the interviews occurred when survivors and their advocates discussed the failure of the Church to be what it professes itself to be. For some, the hypocrisy involved observations about the disjuncture between what the Church professed and what it practiced; for others, it had more to do with reflections on the Church's teachings.

Do as I Say, Not as I Do

One of the central themes that survivors talked about in their relationships to the Church was the realization that it had violated some of its own teachings. Survivors often used the tool of juxtaposition to demonstrate what they perceived to be the duplicity of the Church. One survivor captures this stark contrast cogently as he discusses the Church's continual stonewalling before and during his litigation:

> By coincidence, the bishops came out with one of their pastoral messages right around the same time [as I confronted the Church], and it had to do with the sexual abuse of children ... It was called, "Walk in the Light" or something like that. It was a pastoral message saying that abuse of children was wrong, including abuse within the Church. I forget the exact details, but it was something to the effect that it was important for people to speak freely about this and for abusers to be held accountable and so on. And I thought, "What a bunch of hypocrites!" Because this is what they are saying publicly, but in private *this* [points to the gag order initiated in the litigation] is what they are saying [in private].

Others cite similar themes of utter disgust with hypocrisy:

> The deepest part of my anger—and I said this to my parents—is the [slowly, for effect] self-righteous piety with which they traversed all of this and presented themselves while pure evil was going on. I feel like,

[pause] like I've gone to hell and it's been the Catholic Church. And I feel a moral—*moral* obligation to cut away at it any chance I get. Even if that means challenging every Catholic I run into, their affiliation or their spirituality or whatever. (Douglas)

And [the priest] started with this sermon, and the sermon was about how we as Catholics need to follow the rules. It wasn't that blunt, but that's what it was. Like we should be abstaining before we go to the communion, we should be going to confession, we shouldn't be getting married and divorced. I'm like, "You've got to be shitting me!" And he never said anything about all the rules the Church has broken. The most sacred rules of all. (Jeff)

I'm not saying this against [Pope John Paul II] personally. He's probably a good man. But he's not God … When he went around St. Peter's Square in that pope mobile, I was sick to my stomach at the way they built him out to be God. Talk about false idols! That is not correct. I'm sorry; that is not spiritual. (Fred)

[A high ranking Church official said to me:] "You know what, money—it doesn't solve anything." I [thought], "You pompous ass. You're sitting here at a 16 foot mahogany table, surrounded by Hummels, in a multi-million dollar mansion." (Andrew)

Advocates also shared much of this anger:

You have purported [sic] the most moral entity in the world, acting the most immorally. There is no excuse. There is absolutely no excuse. There is no excuse that they won't even acknowledge that these acts were committed. I mean, it's just terrible, terrible, terrible … They just go on and on … [quietly] I could sit here and tell you sad stories, all disgusting stories, [loudly] *by this moral entity* that is espousing morality while they are raping children or allowing children to be raped, or turning their backs on children. (Zach)

In a similar vein, several survivors talked about how rigid the Catholic Church had seemed during their own upbringing, what they perceived as threatening eternal damnation over small infractions, like eating meat on Friday during Lent, or missing Mass. Many survivors described a general fear of doing something for which they would be eternally punished. Anna talks about this specifically:

For me, growing up, Church was family and family was Church. But we were also taught that if you weren't Catholic you were going to hell. There were indulgences that you could say. You were going to go to hell if you had a mortal sin on your soul before you got to confession. You know, you were on your way to hell.

Moreover, when the Church was confronted with grievous sins of its own priests, the response was often the opposite of what survivors expected and inconsistent with the Church's own teachings. For instance, Virginia talked about being distressed when the bishop's response to her allegation of clergy sexual abuse was, "Poor Father X. He's had such a rough time." Rather than characterizing the priest's sexual advances to her at the age of twelve as inappropriate and sinful, she was instead given this response that seemed totally inconsistent with her understanding of Church teaching about sexuality.

Francis relays an account of being confused over the duplicity of what the Church taught about sexuality and his abuse:

> Just a few months after [the abuse] happened I went to confession at [Church name]. And, um, you know, if you're seventeen and you have two hands, masturbation is going to be one of the first things that you mention. And the priest *ripped me* and told me that I'd committed a mortal sin. A mortal sin is an act that completely severs you from God permanently. That's a *big* deal. Then he told me that I was sick and should get some counseling. So now I'm on the train going back to college, trying to figure out why—17-years-old, good as gold, pure as the driven snow, not drinking, not doing any of that stuff—and I just got reamed for this, when [the priest] tried to [molest me] … Try to make sense of that!

Perceptions of fraudulence chipped away at the legitimacy of the Church in the eyes of survivors. This erosion sometimes occurred in memorable epiphanies, such as those described by Francis, and sometimes through a series of smaller moments of stark juxtaposition between the contemporary Church and the Church they believed in as children. Connie sums up what many survivors probably felt:

> I don't think that they came close to ever being what I grew up thinking the Catholic Church was, as far as being a loving organization.

Do as I Do: Illegitimacy in Religion

In some cases, the rejection of the Church involved a denunciation of both the Church's clear failings (e.g., the lack of oversight for pedophile priests) and actual Church moral positions (e.g., those on abortion, priestly celibacy, etc.). In these cases, the crisis of legitimacy was about Catholic doctrine and theology, not simply about acts by members of the

Church who may have corrupted or misinterpreted the doctrine. Douglas, Greta, and Elise call attention to some of the most biting criticisms of the Church:

> I said to my parents, "Independent of what was perpetrated on our family, the Catholic Church is the most destructive force on the planet. It's about self-deprivation, self-condemnation, guilt, shame. To me it's just a perverted entity. It indoctrinates you at a very young age. It works on nothing but guilt and fear." I recently was with my parents having lunch. I said, "The beauty of the Catholic Church is the simplicity with which it works. If you tell people you have these seven deadly sins, which are actually basic human appetites. The way that you achieve power is to disarm someone. So if you have them wrapped up in trying to control these seven appetites and all that, and if they're not vigilant about it, then, um, they're gonna have eternal damnation. And then the nature of power is to continue to maintain its power ... Then my favorite is the confessional. There's this magic box, it's like, come on in, tell us all your deepest darkest secrets—all your transgressions—and we'll take care of you. What better way than to blackmail people? It's very simple. It's about disarming people, controlling them." (Douglas)

> And now I say: You can't be in a good chapter of the Klan ... [trails off]. Yes, the Church mixes evil with good. Because if they didn't they wouldn't have gotten away with it for so long. And that's exactly what makes this so powerful: that the Church has done good. But now with their virulent explicit efforts to deprive people of their rights, you know, lobbying against equality for gay people, and coming out with the latest diatribe against women, and also continuing to cover-up so much criminal activity ... (Melissa)

These positions reject the actual teachings of the Church.

Shame and the Role of Disclosure

The importance of shame cannot be underscored enough when considering motivations for this type of litigation. Whether defined as a lowering of self-esteem through consciousness of guilt or expectations of social degradation, the notion of shame plays an important role. Briefly, when shame is mentioned by survivors or their advocates, it is mentioned as a disintegrative emotion, involving the rejection of the individual as someone inferior, or, in Goffman's terms, "spoiled." Generally, shame is an emotion that emanates from others' responses or potential responses to a particular action. Although notions of social distance and illegitimacy help elucidate the position that many survivors were in prior to litigating, the "buried" shame (Scheff 1991) that many survivors experienced provided the fuel for many to move forward against the Church. This notion of shame is incredibly complex: although it sometimes involved a feeling that was produced during interaction with an audience, more often, it was a feeling provoked by anticipation of disclosure and accompanying expectations of rejection and alienation. The internal dialogue produced shame, which, in turn, crept into many aspects of survivors' lives, often negatively affecting them in social relationships and other intimate arenas.

To be clear, more than half of the survivors told no one at the time of the abuse (fourteen out of twenty-two). Advocates similarly reported that most of the survivors they knew had not disclosed the experience when it occurred. But even though they did not speak about the experience, the internal rehearsal of disclosure haunted them. The anticipated reaction shaped the meaning of the experience for many survivors.

For those who did disclose to adults (five out of twenty-two), the revelation was usually perceived to be of little consequence; those to whom they disclosed assumed that life would proceed as if the abuse had not happened. Perhaps because most disclosures occurred in the sixties, seventies, and eighties, prior to societal awareness of the harm or long-term consequences of sexual abuse, there seemed to be little understanding that such an experience could cause trauma or shape a person's world view.

The following sections discuss disclosure. First, I examine disclosure at the time of the abuse to authorities and to peers, followed by a discussion about those who did not report at the time of the abuse, as well as those who reported later in life to either the Church or to others.

Those Who Told Adults at the Time of the Abuse
Five of the survivors I spoke with revealed the abuse—actually made a claim—to someone who potentially could have taken action against the priest. In these cases, the process of disclosure becomes important, and the justice, or more precisely, the injustice of the interaction facilitated a transformation of the dispute.

Two survivors disclosed to their parents when they were in middle school in the late sixties. They disclosed together (along with two other survivors not in the study), anticipating that their audience would be more likely to accept the truth of the allegations if multiple boys reported similar events. One of the men recounts this disclosure:

It was a big leap of faith. But I needed three other guys there also to verbalize it; I could not have done that alone, to my father or any other man. Somehow with four of us it was different. We were probably all at a point where we couldn't take it.

Perhaps because of their unified accounts, in this instance, their parents did believe them and went to the diocese to try to force some action by the Church against the offending priest. The priest was eventually moved; but they later learned that he simply had been shuffled off to another parish without any treatment.

However, most stories of disclosure in earlier decades did not end so favorably for the survivor. More often, the victim was made to feel that the abuse was either his or her fault, or that it was something that shouldn't be discussed. Elise relates the following story about what happened when her brother, who was also abused by a priest, tried to get help from relatives:

He was always drunk. Always drunk. He was somebody that was drunk all day, every day. And he told everyone [about the abuse by the priest] and everyone just said, "You've got to sit up straight when you're drinking." The idea was that, in our family, of course, you had to learn how to drink. And if you learned how to drink, you wouldn't say these embarrassing things.

Several advocates relayed stories of clients who had attempted, unsuccessfully, to tell their parents, and who were blamed for the incident. One advocate relayed an account of a priest holding a victim responsible for the incident. Instead of disabusing him of childish notions of self-blame, the priest reinforced them:

There was another man that I knew that tried to tell this other parish priest in confession. ... He said he was confessing his sins to Father X ... And he was an altar boy. And he said, "Father ... I'm thinking about things I shouldn't be thinking about ... there is somebody that is touching me." Nowadays, the priest would say, "You can tell me who it is. I'm going to help you. I want to help you. It's ok to talk about this." Father X just kind of sent him off to do his penance and didn't follow up! And then [it happened a second time and] he told him to do it again a second time. (Janet)

Marilyn, the third survivor who spoke up at the time of the abuse, disclosed to a psychologist whom she had been seeing for panic attacks. She believed that the psychologist believed her, but no action was taken against the priest; authorities were not notified and no complaint was formally filed.

Francis, the youngest of the survivors, was abused in his late adolescence. After one occasion when the priest made inappropriate advances to him, he spoke to his mother, whom he characterized as supportive, and a few months later he contacted the diocese. The response was disappointing:

> I didn't have that much direct contact with [the Church]. I know that I offered to—I told [the Church official by phone] that I would gladly meet with him or anybody when I was home [from college] and the word I got back was that that wasn't necessary and just to write it down and send it in. [slowly] I wasn't particularly thrilled with that answer. In the end, if you want to say that that was one of the many things that led to my litigation, you could definitely say that. ... I wished that they had taken it more seriously. Plus, I don't know, for me it would have been a good experience to meet with them, with somebody. And looking back at that now, they are actually supposed to do that.

Francis felt dismissed by this experience. Although Church officials formally responded, he felt they never truly wanted to learn the truth or to attempt to rectify the situation.

Finally, Lewis, one of the youngest survivors interviewed, had a disastrous disclosure experience after experiencing ongoing abuse for a year. Upon telling his mother about the abuse, she responded, "Don't tell anybody or they'll think you're weird!" While his parents eventually made a complaint to the diocese, the situation went from bad to worse. Lewis was sent by the diocese to a counselor in another state, which made him feel "strange" and "at fault" for what had happened to him. Of the interaction with the Church, he states, "It was like they would dig a hole, throw you down, and then fill you in." In the end, the disclosure was extremely disruptive to both Lewis and his family, and critical in understanding how he came to view the Church as unjust.

In summary, of the five survivors who spoke to an authority figure about the abuse, only two of them succeeded in getting some action against the priest, and even then, they learned decades later that the action was simply to move the priest to another parish, where he continued to offend against children. Marilyn's disclosure was discrete and somewhat neutral; no action was taken against the priest. Francis and Lewis were the only two to confront the Church at the time of the abuse, and those interactions were largely negative.

Those Who Talked to Friends

Five survivors talked to peers at the time of the abuse. Only one of these survivors, Virginia, spoke to peers who were not abused[1]. This encounter was disastrous. Virginia told her friends, somewhat innocently, about the attention she was getting from the handsome new priest who came around courting her while she was in junior high school. Her friends' reaction—mortification—was crushing to her. After the disclosure, the girls no longer associated with her. Of the four other survivors who spoke to peers at the time of the abuse, Fred and Edward talked about vague jokes that their parochial school class would make about the priest being "queer." Both stated that they made up songs about being abused as a way to handle the stress, but never talked to one another in any depth about the pain they experienced. Both Isaac and Lawrence relayed talking to friends whom they knew were also being abused by the same priest. Neither described the conversations as particularly important, except to say that they knew they weren't alone in the abuse; there was someone else in the same situation.

Those Who Remained Silent

Most of the survivors I spoke with (fourteen of twenty-two) told me that they had told no one at the time of the abuse. Of these survivors, all but Henry—who spoke to someone a few years after—waited decades to tell anyone. Advocates confirmed that the majority of their clients had not disclosed abuse for many years.

Greta, Andrew, Douglas, Matthew, Anna, Beth, George, Henry, Elise, Howard, Christopher, Norman, Rick, and Connie did not speak to anyone about the abuse until years later. Greta, Anna, Beth, Douglas, and Connie reported that the abuse had been repressed for some period of time. Greta, Douglas, and Beth's memories were triggered when stories about priest abuse ran in the media. Anna, Beth, and Connie were in therapy when the abuse memories surfaced. The remaining survivors stated that they were aware of the abuse, but did not want to disclose it out of shame or fear.

Why did so many remain silent? Being afraid that one wouldn't be believed is a central consideration for many sexual abuse victims (Dunn 2010). According to victim accounts, most were acutely aware of the power asymmetry[2] in the relationship between priest and child, of both their own low status, as well as the semi-divine status of the priest. This convinced many that no one would believe them. The significance of this relationship cannot be underestimated, as its bearing on the interpretive process of the child is, as two advocates aptly put, "haunting." One survivor described the priest as "the God of my town." Relaying a story of one client, Janet, an advocate, says:

> [The survivor] just couldn't say the words. He couldn't say the words, "Father X is abusing me." He couldn't say the word "Father X" because he knew he was saying something bad about a priest!

Matthew cogently illustrates the differential in power and status involved in the relationship between child and priest:

> ... during that time—1977—priests were next to God. Their word came from God. You couldn't question them. Besides the fact, I'd already had a history with my parents where they'd never believe what I said anyway. One time I was hit by my teacher at school and they said, "Oh, you must have deserved that, go back and get another one." I certainly wasn't going to tell them about this.

Marilyn echoes this, and adds how her abuser was particularly charismatic:

> I didn't want to report him for a couple of reasons. Number one: Everybody loved this guy ... He was very popular. And then the second one: in the years of my abuse, I was very vulnerable. He was very charming and influential. And he convinced me that he was a good friend to me, it was helping me. Even though it was destroying me.

Liam explains the very real fear that others would never believe his story, as well as his understandable desire to suppress the memories in order to escape the pain of what happened:

> I just took it on the chin. Who the hell was going to believe me? My friends? Nobody. Do you want to tell that story? I don't want to tell that story. I want to be *miles away* from that story. Nobody is going to believe it anyway. Who wants to tell it? A pimple at that age is bad luck ... I couldn't tell my mother.

Similarly, Elise explained that she and her brother, who was also abused, were viewed as incorrigible by most adults, and that their status doomed them to not being believed. She drank heavily in adolescence, perhaps as a way of coping. Her status as a troublemaker tarnished any potential credibility she might have had.

While the internal dialogue about being believed was important, a second disincentive came as a result of the specific dynamics from the sacrament of confession. Beyond simply not being believed, survivors of priest abuse can be held hostage spiritually in the sacrament of confession. In this ritual, it is believed that the priest absolves the confessor of his or her sins, washing away the soul, readying it and preparing it to be closer to God. In Catholic dogma, this exercise is one of very few ways to unburden one's soul of impurity and sin; and the priest is the intercessor in this process. Tragically, when this ritual is experienced with an abuser, sins admitted to the offending priest in confession could potentially be used against the survivor. Howard relays this feeling of potential emotional blackmail:

> He's got it on me, man. He knows everything I've ever done that is wrong. I am *screwed*!

For these survivors, the spiritual side may be even more confounding: since the priest is the person with special status to absolve sins, the youth may have believed that disclosure could have damned him eternally to hell.

A third powerful disincentive comes as a result of gendered expectations. Gender was discussed as a major reason for remaining silent. Both the men and women in the study acknowledged a gendered response to victimization, with men having different burdens due to social stereotypes about masculinity. Several men talked about not being able to come forward because they felt that people would tell them they "should have fought him off." In our culture, victimization is more often aligned with female emotions: vulnerability, sadness, etc.; a male victim, as part of masculinity, is expected to be strong and stoic. Fred captures the "indications" he made to himself (Blumer 1963), the symbolic meaning of being both a man and a victim. He explained that men whom he knew around town would avoid greeting him after his abuse was publicized on the front page of the local paper, and he discussed his ambivalence about being known as a victim:

> Why would I want to be part of this group, or movement? We're all branded as victims of sexual abuse! 'Cause the old thing in my mind is that I should have been able to push him [the priest] away. "How could you have let this happen to yourself?" That's what all these other men are saying—or not saying—when they don't talk to me. That's what I'm hearing. And you've got to go through that. And I went through that.
>
> I had my friends tell me, [incredulously] "Why didn't you kick him in the balls?" I says [sic], "You don't get it!!"

Another powerful disincentive is the fear of being labeled a potential abuser (Offen et al. 1997; Mendel 1995; Gerber 1990). Survivors were very aware of the stereotype that those who are abused eventually abuse others. Both Lewis and Henry talked emotionally about fearing other family members' reactions to hearing about the abuse. In Henry's case, his fears were unfounded; his family trusted him and responded in a kind, caring manner when he disclosed as an adult. In the following passage, he discussed symbolic indications to himself in the transformation of the experience:

> And I had gone to visit my brother three times to try to tell him [about the abuse], and I just couldn't. And so the third time I went I, came home and ... I realized on the way home that the reason that I hadn't been able to tell them was because they had ... sons [he breaks down crying here] and I was afraid that they would suspect me of child abuse and they wouldn't want me to ... [through tears] they wouldn't trust me with their children. That wasn't at all true. When I finally worked up the courage to tell them, they immediately understood that fear and didn't agree with it. They didn't feel that way at all. But that was *huge* and still is.

Lewis' family, however, was not nearly as understanding. He reported that one family member restricted his access to his children, fearing that his history of abuse would cause him to become an abuser himself, a feature of his current situation that caused him a great deal of pain.

Women encountered a separate set of problems when dealing with victimization. Lynne, an advocate, talks about their different coping mechanisms and motivations:

> The women were going to support groups, and the men were hiring lawyers. [slight laugh] I don't think there's a lack of female victims out there, I just think they are coping differently. From the ... group [I know], I know they did. If you were raised Catholic, women have a very different role in the Church and some of them were told, in no uncertain terms, "Look chaste. Look pure. Don't distract father so-and-so from his calling. Anyone who does is a slut and a whore." So they're dealing with all that.

Because so many victims believed that they could not tell anyone, the emotions and confusion of the experience were left to fester within their own self-dialogue, resulting in "buried shame" (Sheff 1993). This shame often translated into feelings of personal defectiveness. Not only were victims convinced that no one would believe their stories, but also they felt that they had been selected for abuse because of some inherent badness within them. This left many victims believing that he or she was the only one to whom this had happened. Although survivors talked about their individual battles with shame, all of the advocates in the study talked about the patterns they observed among their clients who had remained silent about the abuse. Janet speaks to this directly when asked why so many people did not come forward about the abuse earlier:

> Because they thought they were the only ones. They were ashamed and felt that they did something wrong to bring this upon themselves ... I mean, they still had virtually no self-esteem, because, you know, this had been going on for years ...

Lynne recounted the felt isolation of many of the victims with whom she worked:

> And for years the Church wouldn't tell them there were others. They went through their whole life thinking, "I'm the only one. He picked me. There is something wrong with me."

All of the advocates I spoke with shared stories of victims contacting their offices for information about other victimizations by a particular priest, with no intention of filing a lawsuit.

> And so, some people were just calling for information: "Do you know if there are other victims of father so-and-so? It's important to me to know." ... We would tell them without using any names, "Yes, we've been in contact with other victims. There are other victims in the world." (Lynne)

Trevor, another advocate, talks about his initial conversations with clients in which he discusses the ramifications of sexual abuse:

> And then they'd start telling me about their lives. And then I'd look at them and say to them, "If you've gone through this, you know what that makes you?" And people would brace themselves—and I'd say, "Normal." [with drawn out emphasis on every word] "That's the normal, expected response of victims of childhood sexual abuse." And they would just cry. People would just cry. Because for a lifetime, they had been convincing themselves that they were fucked up. You know, to put it bluntly. *That there was something wrong with them*, that they were devalued human beings ... And to hear what they had gone through before they even said it, and to hear somebody say to them,

"You're normal," was an incredibly difficult thing for a lot of people to hear, and an incredibly difficult thing for them to process. And that triggered a lot of recognition that they could get help. That it was ok to go to someplace to work through this. Because, you know what? They were a normal person [sic] dealing with an abnormal event.

Adult Disclosures to the Church

Many of the survivors disclosed or made some sort of claim decades after the abuse occurred, and often the responses they received justified earlier fears. These interactions were often some of the most defining for survivors: their earlier fears about not being believed were realized, and they were often left feeling isolated and violated. In these interactions, which were more frequent than disclosures during childhood, the role of audience (Mather and Yngvesson 1987) and the elements of procedural justice (Tyler 1993; Lind and Tyler 1988) and shaming (Braithwaite 1993) become very relevant. All of the interactions discussed in this section involve disclosures that occurred prior to any litigation. Usually, these disclosures served to fuel the "slingshot effect" of intensifying any dissatisfaction the survivor may have had.

As Braithwaite notes, justice interactions have the capacity to be either inclusive or exclusive (1997). In this study, many survivors (e.g., Lewis and Francis) found themselves locked out of their faith community with responses from the Church hierarchy that were perfunctory at best, and at worst, intimidating and exclusionary. The responses that survivors encountered are worth elaboration, as many directly identify the disintegrative processes, the exclusionary mentality, and the overall lack of procedural justice. Although several survivors did relay more recent positive pastoral responses in their interactions with the Church, in general, the pre-litigation interactions served to draw lines in the sand between the Church and the victims.

Some survivors reported there were some interactions which lacked any subtlety and clearly fall into the category of egregious violations. For instance, Elise talks about her initial efforts, prior to any litigation, to get her offender pulled out of service with children:

The first thing that [the Church] said to me is, "We will destroy you." That was their *first response*. All I said was, "Please keep Father X away from children." I even said "Please!" You know? And their immediate response was, "We will destroy you. We will take you down in public."

With the subtlety of a sledgehammer, such a response violates the premises of procedural justice. Henry illustrates a second example of how he and the Church became adversaries during one interaction:

> [After our first meeting, the Bishop] said he'd get back to me. Of course, I didn't hear from him for a while. About a month later, I called him and we went in again to see him. And he told me that they had got the evaluation, that the priest had "sexual issues" but that they didn't feel he had a deviant personality, and they intended to place him back in ministry. [short pause] I kind of lost it. He said the priest denied that any of this happened. And I said, "Are you saying you don't believe me?" He said, "I'm saying that the priest denied that it happened and we believe him." But he would never say he didn't believe me. So I started to get angry. And I started yelling. Then he started to get angry and then [he] started yelling back at me. And then he started saying, "If your intention was to get me angry, well, you've succeeded." And he [laughs] was quite perturbed that he was angry— that *he* was! And accusing me of sort of somehow got him angry and setting him up. They continued to say they were going to put him back in ministry. At that point, I said I was going to pursue this another way. He asked me what I was going to do, I said I didn't know, "Maybe I'll sue you, maybe I'll go to the newspaper. I don't know." So I stormed out.

In this example, the issue of correctability becomes paramount. Henry saw that his attempts to make the Church respond were fruitless. He further alludes to the eventual litigation as the only means to force the Church to respond. While these interactions overtly drew battle lines about the roles of the survivors and the Church, others were more subtle. Francis talked about the Church's minimization of his allegations, and his desire to have the Church take the incident more seriously:

> I got a letter back—not from the bishop—who was actually in charge at the time—but from [another priest] at the Pastoral Support of Priests office ... It was really good and really bad at the same time. It was good because they made a point to say that all of my reactions were normal and healthy. I did everything that I was supposed to—I didn't do anything wrong. And that sort of stuff. So that was good. But they also kind of minimized the whole thing. They said, "Priests aren't supposed to bring anybody up to their bedrooms or their personal quarters, and therefore, that was wrong." They didn't acknowledge any of the other stuff that happened and described everything as my "discomfort." Looking back on it, I can see it's a very minimizing thing, and it framed how I looked at it for a *long* time after that.

Rick discusses how the priest he approached tried to minimize the abuse:

> We went to Father X, who knew me since I was a kid. And he married us. I said, "I have to speak with you." He said, "What's on your mind?" I said, "Well, it's kind of personal." He said, "Come on down tomorrow at 4." I go to see him. He said, "What's on your mind, Rick?" I said, "I was raped by Father D as a boy." He has this big chair and he rolls over [and leans in]. He said, "Well, how old were you?" So I tell him. He said, "That was a long time ago, Rick. Time has a way of playing on things, you know. Did it really happen?" I said, [incredulously] "What?" He said, "Well, not that it didn't happen, but sometimes your mind has ways of playing ... maybe it's exaggerated, maybe it wasn't that bad, or maybe it was worse." I said, "What are you saying, Father?" He said, "I'm just saying, it was a long time ago, Rick. Why are you bringing it up now?" I said, "Why?" [He responds:] "I have a half hour. It's ten past four." I said, "No, it's time I went."

A few survivors relayed accounts where the Church's response was to pity the offender:

> I got a call from the Archbishop in the diocese telling me how, "Poor Father X, he had such a rough time. Poor Father X was a drunk." Like basically, 'How could *you* do this to *poor Father X*?' (Virginia)

Anna also talks about some of the more subtle aspects of procedural justice that also have consequence. In this interaction, she demonstrates the importance of non-verbal language:

> So I wrote a handwritten report ... And I brought some other pictures and some poetry. And [the victim liaison] forgot I was coming! So I arrived at this horrific ... building—because that's where you met ... I don't know if you've been inside [that building]. It's really very cold, the actual office. The safety issues around it—it's like a bank. There's a lot of bullet proof glass ... So she came out. I had called to confirm the day before and to tell her I was still coming. I didn't talk to her, but I left a voice message. So I'm sitting there, and I'm a wreck ... So we sat in like this classroom—I don't know what it was—and she never even shut the door! Fortunately, my friend Jane got up and said, "Can we shut the door?" ... She was an older woman nun. She was outrageous. But I also have heard from other survivors that she could be very vicious. She was not vicious with me, she was just like I just didn't *exist*. I mean, she just like, annihilated me as far as not even remembering that I was coming. I did write a letter about it with suggestions with how to handle survivors. Had I not had the experiences and the education and the support I had that would be a

very upsetting experience, for somebody to be forgotten. So I wrote a follow-up letter. She never passed anything on. When I finally went again to the church, they couldn't find anything in a file. They couldn't. So I had to present it all over again.

Although the interaction suggests some problems with voice, it also suggests a more subtle component of procedural justice which Tyler and Levanthal did not identify: empathy. Lacking in Anna's account of confronting the Church is any sense of humanity or personal connection on the part of the listener. At no point did Anna feel that the liaison was really interested in understanding her pain. Through both the fortress-like physical space issues, as well as the non-verbal cues she picked up, Anna felt that the Church representative did not care.

Another survivor, Lewis, talks about a similar encounter with the Church's victim liaison. In this encounter, the liaison eventually found his file, after spelling his name wrong, looked through it, then, grimacing as she read it, said in a patronizing tone: "Ooohhh. I'm *real* sorry." With her sitting behind a desk piled high with files of other cases of sexual abuse, Lewis began to pick up on the subtle reality: people's lives had been reduced to disorganized files; and the insensitivity of it all left him absolutely deflated and devalued. Again, the issue of lack of empathy is germane. He began to feel powerless and frustrated. At that point, Lewis threatened to sue. The representative immediately reminded him that he couldn't, because he had signed a waiver in his previous visit[3]. The short interaction left the seeds of defiance; his response was, "I'm going to laugh in your face someday."

Similarly, Beth talks about her interactions with the Church:

But then [the victim liaison] never would return phone calls. [The liaison] actually called me abusive ... because I was demanding that [the liaison follow through with what he or she agreed to do, such as contacting the pastor] ... Needless to say, two years back and forth— and all I wanted was for them to pay for my therapy. I didn't want to sue or anything. Maybe three years. Finally, it had to be where [my family] was threatening a lawsuit, so that they would pay for therapy. What they said was, I obviously had a supportive family and had the means, and so I didn't deserve to be paid for.

In a slightly different twist with the same implications of essentially being denied standing or the opportunity to represent oneself, George relates his experience of attempting to contact the [Church] both to obtain money for therapy, as well as to create a safe place for other survivors within the Church. Each time, he was rebuffed:

> So anyway, they said no, letter after letter, phone call after phone call, blowing me off after blowing me off, not responding, not responding, not responding. I finally went down to the [Church] and met with the social worker there. I told him my needs. And basically there was a point where I was pushed—or actually, more like threatened or challenged—to file a lawsuit. I told him, "I need money for therapy." He said, "George, you can hire a lawyer and file a lawsuit." So I did!

Despite George talking about money as a factor, the sting of the stonewalling clearly had some bearing in his decision. At no time in his interactions with the Church did he feel he was being taken seriously. Having given up hope that the Church would respond to his satisfaction, he decided to litigate.

Below, Connie discusses how omissions can be experienced as unjust. Here, she describes her first contact with the Church about her offender, a priest later identified as a chronic pedophile:

> I called the Church really early on, about a few weeks after I started to remember. I called the diocese, and asked them where he was. They told me he was in prison. And I was like, "What do you mean? What did he do?" And they said, "Well, he was molesting children." They didn't say, "Why are you asking?" I said, "Is he getting help?" They said, "We have no idea what his program is." And I said, "Well, don't you care? Will he be a priest?" And they said, "Well, we don't know what we're going to do at this point." And they didn't ask for any information from me! ... And I was really disappointed by that.

While at first the omission may sound like a benign mistake, it reaffirms the lack of interest that people within the Church demonstrated, validating fears that many victims held in silence for so long. Again, the interactions demonstrated a lack of empathy for the victims on the part of the Church.

Each of these interactions represents a turning point for the survivors in how they viewed their relationship with the Church. In each case, the survivors approached the Church in hopes of working cooperatively, and left as outsiders. They were also reminded that the Church they had been brought up in had effectively turned its back on them, perhaps when they needed it most. Norman, a survivor and advocate, poignantly sums up many victims' sentiments:

> We absolutely thought that if we told a priest, a bishop, a vicar general—anyone from the Church—that they would jump on this situation and do what was right. They could have prevented the

litigation in 90 percent of the cases if they had given a simple, decent, human response to the victims.

In summary, these descriptions present clear procedural justice problems. Survivors were upset not only with the outcome of the interaction, but also with how they were treated. Their stories relayed a consistent theme that empathy was notably lacking. Particularly when Anna talks about the Church's victim liaison forgetting her appointment and then not closing the door during this sensitive meeting, or when Henry speaks about the Church representative getting angry with him for following up on his abuse complaint, victims realize that their needs did not register with the Church. Their opportunity to represent themselves was corrupted, despite the willingness of Church officials to meet with them. Although issues of ethicality and impartiality were important to survivors, the components of correctability and voice clearly trumped other concerns. When survivors realized that they had hit a stone wall in terms of being listened to or having any action taken (e.g., pulling the offender out of ministry with children, getting the offender therapy, having their own therapy paid for, etc.), these experiences, described usually in great detail, were often turning points in the transformation of their disputes.

Adult Disclosures Outside the Church

Survivors received multiple messages from close family or friends when they disclosed in adulthood. These responses ranged from extremely compassionate to brutally insensitive. In fact, many survivors reported experiencing a variety of reactions. While Virginia's family was accusatory and callous, others supported her:

> But I've seen a lot of kindness. To see how these people *believe* it's phenomenal! It's very touching. When I've gone to some of these [demonstrations], all these people that believe in something. Because you spent so long thinking you were alone and bad and all that stuff.

Many received the message, particularly from older relatives, that the abuse was something that it was best not to talk about. Greta relayed a story of how when she disclosed (as an adult) to her father, he admitted to being abused by a priest as well, but that he had moved beyond it:

> Even though he said he believed me I felt almost discounted, like he didn't know. He acknowledged it, which was different than my mother, but it was almost like it was insignificant. Like, well, 'It happened to me and I moved on and proved to them that I'm gonna

[sic] be successful.' And he was, he was successful in his career … It was all discounted. It was a weird kind of thing. He believed me, but it wasn't like it was that important. I was making too big a deal of it maybe …

In the following interaction, Lawrence relays how his father's response created a "slingshot effect" (May & Stengel 1990):

So anyways, I told my father that this had happened to me and I thought that it was important that this priest was molesting kids in [our state] in the sixties because he wasn't dealt with properly, and that's why so many kids got molested by him in [subsequent decades] in other parts of the country. [quietly] And my father just had a fit, raked me over the coals. Just really insulted me and guilt-tripped me and accused me of essentially *bringing scandal to my family*. And so I said to him, "You know what? You weren't there to protect me when I was a kid. There's a difference now, I'm all grown up. I can do it for myself. I don't care what you think. The story is coming out tomorrow." And that was the beginning of … years of fights and animosity. He did everything he could to stand in my way to prevent me from speaking out, to prevent me from reaching out to other victims, to prevent me from embarrassing him, as he told me over and over, I was embarrassing him. He couldn't walk down the street and hold his head up because he was so embarrassed. So that's what I stepped into when I decided to go public! [laughs]

Howard talks about how some folks still don't understand the gravity of the abuse and its crippling effects on the survivor to reach out:

A woman said to me one time, she sat there and said to me, you know, "Why didn't you tell anybody?" I said, "Take this for a picture: The first person that I kiss is a priest and I'm French kissing him and then embrace and then I start … Are you catching the picture yet?" And I stop going through every detail. [laughing] And she said, [overwhelmed] "That's enough!" And I said, "You can't handle it now, what makes you think you could have handled it thirty years ago? You can't handle that?" I mean, come on? When was it a nine-year-old's job? You've got to be kidding me. You couldn't [even] talk to your kid about [anything sexual] … But you want *that little boy*, at that age, who doesn't even know what sex is, not even mature sexually. 90 percent of us who were abused were abused in pre-pubescent … *We didn't know!* We didn't know because we weren't mature physically or mentally able to handle it. We just knew it was wrong. Let me put some salt and pepper on the top of it for you: [emphatically] A priest? You know, next to God. Some of these priests threatened [the kids]. This guy beat me into submission. I mean, come on.

Pride

The final condition required for the defiant act of litigation against the Church involves defiant pride. Such an emotion occurs when those "ashamed of being ashamed" find cause to feel self-righteous (Sherman 1993, p. 447). For many survivors, the media coverage provided the linchpin in transforming buried shame into defiant pride: when individual survivors discovered that they were, in fact, not alone in being abused, the shame they felt for so many years turned to anger as they began to zero in on the complicity of the Church in moving known pedophiles around instead of removing them from ministry. Survivors came to understand, to greater or lesser degrees, that they were not "defective individuals" but individuals who had been egregiously wronged. The understanding that they were part of a larger group also helped to foster angry pride. Budding victim communities—whether real or virtual—were universal in the clergy sexual abuse litigation I studied. Real communities occurred when people connected with one another as a result of their shared experiences; virtual communities were created when victims came to identify with other victims in the media, although never formally connecting. For instance, Matthew, who had not connected with any other survivors through the course of his litigation, told me that he personally felt connected to another victim whose suicide had recently been reported in the media.

Whether real or virtual, the key was that the individual victims became aware that their abuse had made them part of a larger community. This transformation was a critical one, and one that perhaps has been overlooked in the media. Although victim communities (e.g., those involved in Survivors Network of those Abused by Priests or the Linkup) existed prior to 2002, they were significantly smaller and more localized. One leading advocate stated that membership in SNAP doubled—increasing by several thousand people nationwide—after the scandal broke in 2002. The breadth of this community of victims was discovered in the first half of 2002, and people previously unaware of their commonalities came to understand that they were, in fact, members of a wronged group.

Janet, a victim advocate, talks about the emotions that victims felt as the events unfolded in Boston in early 2002:

> They were ashamed and felt that they did something wrong to bring this upon themselves. And when they saw the numbers out there and started seeing the names of their own perpetrators—and that was healthy—they started to realize, "Wait a minute!" ... they started to say, "There is something wrong here with the whole picture, and maybe, *maybe*, it wasn't my fault." ... They were angry because they felt that, "Not only did he do this to me—not only did he destroy my life—but he's destroyed others" prior to and subsequent to their own abuse.

Whereas prior to 2002, victims may have sensed that there might have been other victims, no one I talked to believed that the scandal involved so many children, priests, and supervisors. In 2002, as many victims "went public," they came to understand that they were not personally responsible for the abuse. Moreover, the growing numbers of people coming forward emboldened the victims who had been "ashamed of being ashamed" for so long (Sherman 1993, p. 447). They shared each other's pain and grew stronger in their opposition to the Church, as they had learned to become angry not only for their own abuse, but also for others' abuse as well. Liam colorfully illustrates this feeling of pride:

> We're a bunch of good Catholic hens that have come home to roost! And we're not leaving. And there is a *huge* ugly, huge army of people that have an axe to grind and they have every reason to swing it and they've got righteousness behind them. You've got to be careful when they come down the hill at you. Cause they got nothing to lose. And that's what I think. And that's what happened. We fought a battle.

While victims who were not involved in the Boston Global Settlement clearly had very different experiences, the elements of social solidarity and defiant pride were critical. Many of these cases involved a smaller group of victims of a single priest coming together (e.g., what happened with Lawrence, Connie, Isaac, and Virginia). Virginia and Isaac reconnected with people whom they had known as children, while Lawrence and Connie became connected with people they came to learn had also been abused by the same priest. Even Christopher, who litigated alone, connected with others whom he knew had also been abused. Matthew was the only victim I spoke with who didn't connect with other victims before or during the process. This concept of solidarity is critical both early in the litigation and at later stages.

The threads discussed here refute rational choice theorists who suggest that litigation is an action taken after weighing measurable risks and benefits. The sense of community with others, the righteousness that people felt, the sense of vanquishing buried shame: these are not the ingredients of a rational calculus model. They lend more support to relational theorists who posit that relationships are paramount in the decision to litigate.

---

[1] Virginia subsequently learned in adulthood through the process of litigation that one of the girls to whom she disclosed had also been molested by the same priest.

[2] Although not quite as wildly asymmetric, the disparity can be compared to that of doctor and patient. May and Stengel (1990) observe that the context of such a relationship discourages any type of disputing (p. 110). If this is true of the patient-doctor relationship, the gravity of the priest-child relationship is likely to be exponentially greater.

[3] Another survivor relayed a similar story about the Church liaison trying to make him sign a waiver to release the Church from liability at an early disclosure meeting.

5
Establishing Truth

They wanted someone to talk with who would believe their story. They thought they were alone until they read the newspaper. Some of them didn't know what their goals were but they had a feeling they had to talk to somebody ... They would come in. Some were police officers. Some were executives. Some wealthy, some not. And many of them wept, because they'd never told their story to <u>anyone</u> including their spouses. So they wanted to reveal it and they wanted something done.
(Richard, a clergy sexual abuse advocate)

The loosening of social bonds and the loss of belief in Church legitimacy created fertile ground for defiance toward the Church. Litigation then became an act of that defiance—an extension of most survivors' established rejection of the rules of the Church (e.g., not attending Mass, not going to confession). During the early stages of litigation, there was little talk about strategy or agenda; the goals were mostly amorphous, but usually had something to do with establishing truth. Using various terminologies, nearly all of the survivors expressed their desire that the truth be exposed. This sense of truth, however, is loaded with both personal and societal implications. While all survivors wanted the truth about the abuse and the pastoral malfeasance established, they focused on different consequences of the truth. Some wanted the truth to be established so they could exorcize the ghosts of their memories or vanquish some of the shame they had carried; others wanted to establish truth to support fellow survivors. Still others wanted the truth known to make the Church bear formal responsibility or to alert the larger community. In many cases, survivors relayed a combination of these motivations. Whatever the underlying motivation, nearly all agreed that the civil system was a last resort for survivors. As one advocate put it,

I think that part of it is that they went to us because there was nobody else to go to. A few of them had tried going to the police. I think that we were all that was left ... I think they felt that they did not know where else to go.

With that in mind, litigation became the vehicle to establish that truth.

Establishing Truth with "Normals": Believing Oneself

Perhaps the most often cited motivation for establishing truth is personal.[1] For many survivors, putting to rest questions about their own memories was paramount, and doing so involved recruiting outsiders to listen and assent to their pasts. This motivation essentially revisits the naming stage within the transformation of disputes. Because this particular type of abuse is utterly dissonant with Catholic values about the role of the priest and sex in general, survivors often could not reconcile their own memories with what they had been taught in a Catholic upbringing. Because the priest is supposed to be a holy man— an intercessor between the lay person and God—the idea that he could violate a child in such a horrible way was nearly unbelievable for many victims. Having worked with hundreds of victims, one legal advocate I interviewed states: "The whole thing is so incongruous and confusing. Sometimes even *they* don't believe it happened." Several survivors confirmed just that: they had trouble believing—essentially "naming"— their own memories. Elise comments on how the mind tries to push out such difficult memories:

> And it's in your interest to deny it. Because how else could you be a sane person? That's the fear, that you'll go crazy. I have to say, even when the [another priest's] case came up in [a few years later], I had this incredible experience. I had not gone forward. I was never going to talk ... And someone from my town had just called me up, this girl I had grown up with. And she said, just nonchalantly, "When I read about that Father X, I realized the real situation with [the priest they knew]. I wanted to call you up." And I was like, "What are you talking about?" I even thought that it was like, a sin to say that! "Ok, see you later, bye!" I could not [deal] ...

This dynamic was powerful, and several victims relayed being unable to qualify or name that experience.

For those who had difficulty believing themselves, their personal identities (Goffman 1963) were in many ways conflicted and unsteady. Judith Herman (1997) discusses the frailty of traumatic memories:

> Both patient and therapist must develop tolerance for some degree of uncertainty, even regarding the basic facts of the story. In the course of reconstruction, the story may change as missing pieces are recovered. This is particularly true in situations where the patient has experienced significant gaps in memory ... they must learn to live with ambiguity while exploring at a tolerable pace (pp. 179-180).

The stories survivors and their advocates shared with me demonstrated the uncertainty that Herman cites as typical of trauma survivors. In the following passage, Beth discusses confronting her own memories:

> When you recall totally repressed memories, there is this awful part of you, this sneaky feeling that, "What if this didn't happen?" Then I have this argument with myself, like, "If this isn't right, why am I making up such a ridiculous thing?" I'd be even more crazy for that! So there is this need for validation. And to go in there [the chancery] and stand there with my [family] beside me was a step toward that.

She proceeds to talk about confronting her memories by literally going back to the place where she was abused:

> I had to go to the church where I grew up ... for [a] funeral. And I went to it and the rectory where [the priest] used to bring me, and it looked different. And I was panicking. And all my fears that what I had remembered might have been false ... And so I had to ask them, "What happened to the stairs?" There was an outside staircase, and they had put an addition on [years later]. I was like, whew!

Howard talks about the moment he finally confronted his memories:

> ... by that time I had put it all away. I was blaming myself. I couldn't understand. I didn't know. Till I watched [a particular movie] ... It isn't until the end of the film when ... [the main character] had been abused ... he didn't want anybody to see him for what he was. There is this whole cathartic thing in the movie. I ended up getting up and vomiting in my toilet in the bathroom because I recognized [him] ... Devastating. To the point where I was physically ill, in the bathroom, vomiting.

In the following passage, Greta talks about the moment when she first confronted her memories:

> And that's when it all came clear to me. I saw [the priest] on the news. I saw the picture of him in handcuffs, which they always show on TV, being led in or out of the courthouse ... And all of a sudden, it was

"Oh my God!" [shudders]. It was unbelievable, because I never knew his face. I don't remember his face as a young man, so it made me think back. But I just *knew* and I ran to the bathroom and threw up ... I found myself on the floor in a fetal position, sobbing, sobbing. Like reliving it almost. Body hurting. And it just all came together. And I knew it was him, and I knew that was—I knew. It was awful. It was terrifying. It was terrifying but it was also a relief, like, ok, all the pieces fit together.

Each of these examples illustrates the instability of the naming stage for many survivors. Douglas, Beth, Greta, and Anna talked specifically about repressed memories. Perhaps more common, though, were suppressed memories—those that survivors knew existed, but had taken some conscious steps to shelve because they were too painful to confront. These survivors did not consider their memories repressed; they were aware of them, but tried not to think about them and kept them secret from others. Given these irreconcilable memories, litigation became a tool to validate their pasts.

Several survivors talked about how seeing other survivors in the media triggered their own memories. Douglas and Christopher reported that watching others in the news prompted them to revisit the naming stage. Here, Douglas talks about the first person to whom he disclosed the abuse after decades of repression:

First, myself. The thing that clinched it for me was my sister talking about the fact that she had been raped. You know, memories of the time that it happened to me came flooding back. I'm not crazy. It did happen. It was happening at the same time, and her talking about it ... I called my brother ... I said, I want you to talk to this individual, who the [newspaper] article mentioned, and I said, "I'm going to describe [the priest's] bedroom to you. I don't want you to say a word. I want you to speak to so-and-so. Just get back to me." My brother called me the next day and said, "You nailed it to the wall." I was able to tell him it was a small, narrow bedroom with a bay window, white walls, white bedspread, white carpeting. If you are looking out the bay window it looks out over the convent of [the] parish. If you're looking at the bay window, the entrance to the bedroom is to your back. I described the bedspread.

Christopher relays a similar story:

The very first person I talked to was ... another kid that I knew. Because I thought I was crazy and I just needed to verify some things with him. Specifically, what the priest's bedroom looked like. And I knew that he knew. So I described it to him, and then he confirmed it. And then I said, "Ok, I'm not crazy."

He goes on to talk about how comforting it was to hear this person verify his own memories, because the events he remembers were so horrible, so unbelievable, that even now he says that for brief moments he sometimes cannot believe his own memory. In that sense, having other people come forward has been incredibly cathartic for him, as it allowed him to finally name his past. For both, these experiences helped to fast forward the transformation of disputes to the blaming and claiming stages, propelling them to the disputing stage quickly.

Believing oneself involved wrestling ghosts to the ground with a safe audience. Because clergy sexual abuse involves so many taboos (e.g., sexual abuse, the role of the priest, same-sex encounters, sometimes older children, etc.), disclosing this type of abuse meant bringing out potentially "discreditable information" to outsiders. As was described in the last chapter, survivors feared that such a revelation could cause others to confer a spoiled identity on them. Because of this, the choice of audience was crucial for survivors; personal injury attorneys who had some experience with these cases proved to be the individuals who were unlikely to view their identity as "spoiled." Goffman (1963) refers to persons such as these as "wise":

> … persons who are normal but whose special situation has made them intimately privy to the secret life of the stigmatized individual and sympathetic with it, and who find themselves accorded a measure of acceptance, a measure of courtesy membership in the clan (p. 28).

This group of attorneys was seen as providing a safe venue for survivors to tell their stories. One legal advocate talks about the dynamic the media exposure set up between survivor and attorney:

> [This attorney] was a very *public* figure. People were connected to him through the media. They perceived him as someone very strong and empathic, as someone who could really help them. (Lynne)

Because of their extensive public appearances in the media, a small group of prominent attorneys was widely recognized in the community. Perhaps as a consequence of that recognition, just three firms represented nearly 75 percent of the clients in the Boston Global Settlement. This is important in that survivors knew that they approached safer ground when they went to tell their stories; the "wise" were less likely to see their pasts as discreditable.

Knowing that their experiences were unimaginable to society, the attorneys proved to have a powerful impact on these victims through the simple act of listening to and affirming their stories. Most advocates described themselves as among the few people in society who did believe the stories, prior to 2002. This element of establishing truth for their own piece of mind clearly played a role in victims' decisions to litigate. Ultimately, those victims who decided to litigate were in some ways taking a blind step in attempting to establish their personal truths, confident enough to engage an outsider and tell their stories, but not yet aware of what the establishment of truth would eventually come to mean in their lives.

In the following passages, two legal advocates from different firms speak very similarly about why people initially came to them:

> We had people come in and say, "I don't even know why I'm here, but I'm here ..." I think that in the beginning what they really wanted was just to have somebody to listen to them and not judge them negatively. And some of our clients, for a long time, were so concerned that we would judge them negatively ... And a lot of our first meetings were just that. Just hearing people ... (Justine)

> They all felt alone. They were all isolated. They didn't think anybody else had been molested. They all thought that they were at fault. They were all ashamed and embarrassed. Their goals, initially, were to have someone listen to their story and believe them. What happened originally was, they would come in one by one and I'd listen to them, and they would all—not all, but most of them—they'd all say the same thing, in the same way. They'd say, "I finally met someone who would believe me. You don't know what a great weight has been lifted off my shoulders." And they all used that phrase: a great weight has been lifted off my shoulders. I find that to be so interesting, that they would use the same phrase. They all would come in saying, "You're not going to believe this." And when they realized that I believed them, and that I knew all about these priests, especially [names a notorious pedophile], many of them just started crying, men and women. (Zach)

These motivations, relayed by both advocates and survivors alike, are consistent with some of the law and society literature that notes that personal goals, such as the assertion of "self worth" (Bumiller 1988) or the expression of personal dignity (McCann 1994), often play a large role in the incentive to sue.

However, not all of the survivors received this support when they contacted an attorney. Casey, who had been raped by a priest who was a confidante to him, talks about the first time he contacted an attorney:

I contacted the law firm. I was actually the first person to contact the law firm about this particular priest. And at the time they said, "Thanks. If you want legal representation, go somewhere else." They didn't believe me either at first. Then a few months later someone else came forward and reported this guy and I called back and the big guy [names a prominent attorney] got on the phone and apologized and said, "I'm so sorry." I'm sure they didn't believe me. Right? His name had never been mentioned before; I was the first person. And at the time, it was still relatively new, the scope of it hadn't become apparent yet. They were being careful ... And as I expected, I wasn't believed.

Many survivors expected not to be believed, particularly by those outside the legal realm. In fact, the majority of the cases in the Boston Global Settlement of 2003 went forward as "John Doe" for that reason: even though these survivors had come forward and talked to an attorney about their pasts, many of them still hadn't told their parents, their spouses, their children, or their employers. In fact, their identities became so crucial that many asserted to their lawyers that they would only litigate if their identities could remain secret. For those who did not go public, their personal identities remained guarded through a process of information control, presenting a different social identity (Goffman 1963)[2].

Establishing Truth about the Nature of the Relationship: Reassigning Blame

Beyond simply being believed, many survivors needed to reassign blame, as several of them had received a variety of messages about their own responsibility in the abuse. As discussed earlier, the transformation of disputes involves a volatile, subjective process. This motivation—revisiting the blaming stage—is particularly important in the context of clergy sexual abuse litigation because of the high levels of initial self-blame involved. Whether survivors articulated this or not, contacting an attorney meant getting an outsider's objective opinion about blame. Being believed was, of course, central. But the difference between contacting a therapist and an attorney lies in the attorney's role as an advocate. In approaching an attorney, survivors hoped to establish their innocence and the other parties' guilt—whether it be the priest or the Church. Not only did it mean they were believed, but also it meant that someone else believed they were wronged so badly that they had a right to demand that the opposing side compensate them for what they had done. Because survivors had received so many mixed messages (e.g., from their families, themselves, the Church) about who was responsible, litigation became a way to draw distinct lines about where responsibility should lie.

Lewis, who had been made a pariah in his family after he disclosed his abuse, talked about going to the lawyer's office desperately needing to hear someone else "pat him on the back" and tell him, "It's not your fault." Similarly, Virginia's family's response—that she was a "whore" who thought she was "God's gift to men"—was so traumatic that she needed others to affirm her lack of blame for the abuse that began when she was eleven years old. Having an attorney take her case helped her shore up a confidence that had been terribly shaken; she no longer needed to accept the blame for what had happened. Similarly, Greta notes, "It was validation that, no, I'm not like a really defective person because I was born that way. There's reasons why I am the way I am." For them, reassigning blame involved vanquishing some of the shame they had carried for years.

Marilyn talks about how the Church attempted to ascribe some portion of blame to her:

> The weird thing about it is that, after hearing about it, he and his other bishops said, "Well, you are a beautiful woman, so we think you deserve 20 percent of the blame." ... They asked me a few times, "Were you in love with him?" And I would say [to the bishops], incredulously: "No. That's not the issue."

Anna talks about her attempt to "give back to the Church what was theirs." She explains that confronting the Church was about displacement of blame:

> Like, I was carrying all the guilt, the responsibility, the secret. And I wanted to give it back to them. It's their responsibility. Because I wanted to give back the shame. I couldn't do that but those were all parts of my process trying to give back. The shame that I carried all my life—the guilt, the self hate—it's *their* shame, it's not my shame. Intellectually, it takes a lot longer to get to it emotionally and spiritually. But sometimes you just act "as if" and eventually, it will fall on them.

Litigation also fostered a reconsideration of the multiple parties responsible. Topping the list of parties at fault was, of course, the Church. Some of the most damnable actions of the Church involved relocating abusive priests so they could prey on other children.

> Meeting the guys in [a nearby town], the next parish he went to ...
> They are four years, seven years younger than me, in their early forties
> to mid-forties. And I'm looking at a group of guys, and then they're
> telling me the *same stories*—only in their parish—about the same guy,
> seven years later, that was groping and grabbing ... And I'm going,
> "Oh my God. This didn't have to happen." My parents tried. I tried.
> This really shouldn't have went beyond ... and there was like
> hundreds of more boys from that, because [this priest] went through
> six other parishes. (Sam)

With Sam, meeting strangers with the same history jarred him, forcing
the realization that the Church had sadly failed in protecting children.
Douglas' experience cut even closer to home. Douglas recounts an
emotional conversation he had with a family member about the guilt he
felt after learning that several other members of his family had been
molested by the same priest:

> [He said to me:] "I could have saved you and [the other members of
> the family]." So I said, "What are you talking about? You were a
> fucking eleven-year-old boy! Who would you go to? Who was going
> to listen to you? I don't accept your guilt. I don't want it. I place the
> blame where it belongs. Not even with [the priest]. I've forgiven him.
> He was a sick man. [The bishop] had no excuse. *He* moved him
> around. They had been well warned."

Elise echoes this, cautioning that despite some of the truly vicious acts
the priests perpetrated, the Church's responsibility was greater still:

> And [the offending priest] would say, "You are making me do this.
> You, you, you: It's your fault. Anything that happens is your fault."
> [stammers] I actually think this is true: Suppose he had gotten
> treatment. You know? Suppose his superiors did not stand in the way
> of him getting treatment. God knows how many children would have
> been protected.

She identifies other parties who also share responsibility and blame for
the abuse:

> [The Church] blamed the hole-in-the-wall doctor [who evaluated the
> priests]. They blamed the family physician. What about blaming the
> county D.A. for failing to contain [this priest]? What about blaming
> [the psychiatrist] who was treating all these pedophiles at [the hospital]
> and letting them out into the community and not reporting them?

Douglas points a finger at the larger Catholic community for not policing its own Church:

> [My sister said to me:] "You sound like you're attacking the Catholic Church." I said, "I am." And she said, "There's [sic] plenty of good Catholics." I said, "No, the Church is the institution. Catholics have a moral obligation to scream for justice, to stop giving money to the Church to clean it right out. If they don't do it, they are an accessory to it."

George widens the net of responsibility to include both his parents and the greater community:

> You know, my parents didn't listen. My neighbors didn't listen. The town didn't listen. Society didn't listen. Our country didn't listen. So, there's a lot of anger that I've had to work through, and a lot of sadness, and a lot of sorrow around the lack of response. Not just from the Church or my personal family unit, but the neighborhood unit, the town unit, the country unit, and the world unit. It's a very sad, sad … [trails off] There was a lot of anger that came up for me. And a lot of sadness. It's really sad that [pause] no one heard my screams and no one responded. We allow this to happen.

Establishing Truth for Other Survivors: Instant Fraternities

Another common motivation articulated by survivors was to assist other victims by coming forward and telling their stories. In almost all cases, survivors talked about either explicitly knowing they weren't the only victims of the particular priest, or sensing that they probably weren't the only ones to be abused. In many cases, an instant fraternity, or sisterhood, was sparked by the disclosure, and a "joint action" (Blumer 1969) was created, with survivors bolstering each other's cases simultaneously. One of the more unique features of this litigation is the social nature that it took on. By identifying with a particular group of victims, or more generally with other clergy sexual abuse victims, survivors felt a stake in making the litigation successful. Several survivors talked about how their inclusion in the litigation would bolster their peers' claims.

Fred talks about the call on his cell phone from a childhood classmate that prompted him to become involved in the litigation:

> [He asked me:] "Would you please come forward? You were instrumental with something in the parish …" He must have caught wind of my mother and father's [actions to notify the Church years

before]. Whatever; I don't know how … And I knew right then, coming off the soccer field. I just knew it had to be stopped. I got a sick sense. I was getting sick. And yeah, I would stand up with [survivor's name]—of course I would. Because this was wrong and it needs to be known.

Lawrence talked about his decision to come forward after he heard that the Church was stonewalling other victims of the same priest:

> … the response from the diocese [to the other victims] was, "How much money do you want? Can we give you some money to shut up about all this?" It was at that point that they realized that they were going to have to take legal action and file the lawsuit, because they weren't getting anywhere with the [names the particular] diocese. And, I said to [another victim], "I'm thinking about maybe I should come forward because all this [abuse] started essentially with me." And he gave me a pep talk and he said that—I forget the exact words now— but something to the effect of, "It's rare that somebody is given an opportunity to really make a difference in the lives of a lot of people. You have an opportunity here. If you decide to go public and step forward, it's going to really mean a lot to a lot of these victims down here." And that was just what I needed to hear.

In a particularly stark moment, one survivor confronted a local bishop with these concerns at a public forum. Here, he describes both his personal needs as well as the need to support other survivors:

> He actually turned and stood there for a minute, whereas usually, he'll come and go. He had his bodyguards around. I asked him to tell the truth. This was early on before the records were opened by the lawyers, before the lawyers got the secret documents unsealed. So we stood facing each other. I started crying. I communicated to him that I was living in limbo, I was living in a vulnerable place of not being able to move forward in my healing because he needed to tell the truth. He needed to open the records. He needed to do his part for the victims who were starting to speak out. He put his hand on me and asked me to pray for him.

Virginia, another victim, was contacted by an advocate who coordinated a survivor group, saying that another victim had come forward alleging abuse by the priest she had named. She immediately told the advocate to give out her phone number, and the two formed a powerful friendship, supporting one another through a difficult litigation process. Isaac shares a similar story: had a childhood friend not contacted him and told him that he was litigating, he states that he might never have filed suit. The friend told Isaac that he might be needed as a witness. At that point, the two friends bolstered each other's litigation with the other's testimony. Similarly, Connie talked about how transformative it was for her when she read in a book about another victim of the same priest: she reached out to both the girl named in the book, as well as several other survivors she came to know about through the process of litigation.

The advocates tell a similar story about survivors wanting to support fellow survivors. Several advocates talked about an outpouring of calls from people—not wanting to litigate—but instead to lend credence to other claims by having their names added to lists of folks abused by a particular priest. This was precisely how Henry began his litigation: he called to offer himself as a witness for others who were to come forward. It was during that call that the attorney suggested that he litigate so that others would see the priest's name in the paper. Although there were complicated motivations, one very clear initial motivation for Henry was to bring out the truth about his priest so that others would be less afraid to come forward, which did occur. In this way, survivors experienced some sort of "bonding" (Putnam 2000) or membership with this new group, whether or not they ever connected with other survivors personally.

Liam talked about his decision early in 2002 to approach other survivors whom he believed had also been abused by the same priest and invite them to informal meetings to talk about their issues. This group quickly coalesced, discussing strategies for litigation and how to support one another through the process. After a few weeks, the group invited an attorney to attend an informational meeting about litigation (and other options) with more than 100 survivors. This meeting later evolved into a weekly support group.

Several of the survivors noted that they realized this newly emerging group was incredibly fragile, and that its positive portrayal in the media was an important goal. In their pursuit, several survivors began strategizing about who should serve as representatives for their group, and they were especially concerned that these individuals appear normal. They did not want a survivor who easily could be discredited acting as a spokesperson. Andrew talks about his decision to see a lawyer after another survivor who seemed unstable came forward in the newspaper:

> Yeah, he looked like a wreck. He was a nervous guy. Then [another survivor] had just gotten arrested ... I said, "My God, they're gonna think these guys are lying because they all look like nut jobs out

there." It's funny because I talked to [another survivor friend] about it and he said he had the same idea. He said, "They need somebody believable. I'm stable; my life is together. I'm not in jail. This really happened. I'm stable and I'm gonna stand up and at least people will be able to identify with the fact that this really happened." ... The story had just broken ... It was to support the guys that were out there. I also knew that I had to do something. You know, there's a time in your life when you've got an opportunity to do something—to say something—I just knew I had to do something or I would never, ever have been able to live with myself.

In the vein of symbolic interactionism, Andrew viewed himself and his friends as credible, believable "normals" (Goffman 1963). These survivors lucidly demonstrate the complexity of presenting oneself as a victim without the negative stigma (Dunn 2010). They believed that the first clergy sexual abuse victims whose stories appeared in the media presented a spoiled identity, and that their representation would not appear credible or normal within society. Andrew and others were concerned that such social representations could malign the entire group. This explicit strategy of information control was an effort to transform the identity of the clergy sexual abuse victim into a credible, normal person. By projecting images of regular guys, they believed they could effectively counter the perceived tendency of the public to discredit information about being abused by a priest. Edward echoes this desire to add credibility to the survivor's stories. After reading the same story Andrew saw in the paper, he observed, "His life was a mess. I knew I needed to do something ... There is only strength in numbers."

Establishing Truth for "Normals": Un-inquiring Minds Need to Know

Establishing truth also involved working to undermine the legitimacy of the Church as a moral institution by "bridging" (Putnam 2000) to the larger community (i.e., having the larger community bear witness to the wrongs perpetrated on the survivors). The goal was essentially to "spoil" the identity of the Church, often with the additional intention of sowing the seeds of prevention. Revelation of the hypocrisy of the Church was on nearly every survivor's agenda. For many, it was a central goal; for others it had less meaning, but was still relevant.

Jeff talks about scripture, ingrained into him as a child, and his new understanding of it as a survivor:

> And [the Church] never said anything about all the rules the Church has broken. The most sacred rules of all … I leafed through the catechism book to see what they said about children and abuse, and all that stuff—and according to their own catechism—which [Cardinal Bernard Law] wrote (he had a part in writing)—it says the greatest sin of all is the sin against a child. It would be better to wrap a rope around your neck … *and* anyone who helps, harbors or enables, yadda yadda yadda, someone to do this, is *worse* than the person who's done this[3]. So how the hell can you …? [trails off] … If they knew … that the Church's number one mission [is], "Feed the hungry. Clothe the naked children." You know, take care of each other. That's what it's supposed to be. And if people truly believe, that's what they're supposed to believe in.

Other survivors cite history to add credence to the idea that the Church was an immoral and corrupt institution. Christopher talks about his efforts to challenge the meaning the Church had for others:

> I've tried to point out to whoever [sic]—members of my family— when you look at the Crusades, when you look at the Spanish Inquisition, when you look at how they turned their back on the Holocaust: What made you think they had any moral authority to begin with?

Howard echoes this theme of setting history right and correcting how others view the Church as a primary motivation for litigating:

> The first thing I said to [my attorney], when he asked me why I was in his office, I told him: "I want systemic and fundamental change for the way these pricks do business." Their tax relief is the biggest dispensation that they have been entitled to. I want no more from them than what I would expect from a corrections officer in a prison, a teacher in a school, a baseball coach in a playing field. I just want the same! We know for a fact that they have raped and pillaged. The world is set up to allow it? Their dispensation is in front of us. We can't even prosecute. And I want them to notice the issue. They are not a moral institution. They are not behaving like one. This is RICO [organized crime]—but it will never become RICO. And they need to be understood, and hopefully for the greater good.

Edward, one of three survivors to remain Catholic throughout most of his life—until he decided to litigate—talks about the Church's callous and calculated responses to its victims:

I'll prove to you that the Catholic Church is still corrupt. Call any church on the South Shore and tell them that you have been abused. The first thing they'll ask about is whether you have a lawyer.

In Attorney J. Minos Simon's memoir about representing the victim in the infamous Gilbert Gauthe case, he notes that the victim's parents' first motivations were articulated as, "It's got to come out. It can't be hidden in the closet anymore," adding, "I want you to bring this out into the light" (1993, pp. 138-139). He sums up their collective motivations, "We remained determined to kick over this rock and show what was beneath it" (p. 142).

Such indictments of hypocrisy and immorality are particularly meaningful to survivors; they want people to understand the Church as a fraudulent and unethical corporate entity that has disregarded human suffering, all the while masquerading as a pastoral institution. Essentially, they have taken on the task of transforming the identity of the Church.

This theme—righting history—was expressed by nearly all of the survivors interviewed, as well as by many of the advocates. Zach, a legal advocate, talks about this topic with particular vitriol:

I could tell you stories on end about how these people's lives changed because of what these people—what these monsters—and what these supervisors allowed to happen. There is no excuse for what the supervisors did. If you can get past what the priest did to the child, how did you get past what the supervisor allowed? [He is almost spitting the next few sentences out:] What kind of monster is that? What kind of disgusting behavior is that? What kind of moral people are these? They are espousing morality all over the place, meanwhile, why don't they look in the mirror? It's not any more complicated than that. It's pitiful.

For many survivors, establishing this truth about the Church was a means to lay the groundwork for prevention efforts. Perhaps one of the most important results of exposing the truth for others to know is that others would then be able to protect their children from predatory priests, and in a broader sense, from any sex offender.

Elise talks about exposing the hypocrisy of the Church as a motivation for litigation. For Elise, the seemingly irreconcilable realities of Church teachings about sexuality and the priest's abuse foment into a complete disillusionment with the institution of the Church. She learned that her offender had been placed in charge of yet another children's institution, despite numerous warnings about his abusive behavior. Such actions—blatantly putting children directly in the crosshairs of a credibly accused pedophile—drove Elise to become outspoken about the duplicity of the Church. After several attempts to deal with the Church outside of litigation, Elise explains that she became strenuously anti-Catholic.

Survivors believed that prevention could be achieved only by outing the truth. Protecting children was a steadfast theme with survivors and their advocates alike, but this goal was acknowledged as a product that could only occur if the truth was established. In other words, a campaign about protecting one's children has no teeth without a history of abuses to build upon. It is these atrocities that effectively wake up outsiders (i.e., "normals") to how the Church processed and coddled sex offenders. Survivors felt that the social reality of the Church must first change; once that was done, prevention efforts could take root.

Establishing Truth for the Church: Shut Up and Listen

Another important facet of establishing truth is forcing the Church to own up to its own history of neglect, surreptitious behavior, and deceit. Survivors felt a strong need to make the Church bear witness to the consequences of their actions. With or without other failed attempts, survivors believed that compulsory legal process seemed to be the only way to make the Church listen. As mentioned in Chapter III, for several survivors in this study, litigation seemed to be the only means of addressing the "correctability" aspect of procedural justice. Stonewalled in their pursuit of justice in earlier claims, several survivors concluded that litigation was the only way to make the Church listen, without turning a deaf ear to their suffering:

> I said [to the bishop], "I don't want any money. I want you to take care of this. I'm not interested in getting anything from you." *The point of going to the attorney was to get their attention back. To say, "You can't just brush me aside."* I really didn't have any other goal other than to confront the Church … I wanted to get involved in this conversation. I wanted a seat at the table … I had always felt that I had allowed my voice to be squelched, and I didn't want that to happen again. I wanted to be able to speak … (Henry)

Similarly, Liam talks about his indefatigable efforts to be heard by the Church that could have prevented his lawsuit had any of his attempts been successful:

> I asked [a Church official], I called him 72 times, I have 72 correspondences before I said, "If you don't meet with me ..." And I went on [television] ... [saying] that I would just drop my lawsuit if he would just open the doors and speak to me. If not, I was going to sue him for $600,000,000—for every cent I could get out of him.

But more than making them listen to their stories, for many survivors litigation was initially about forcing justice upon the Church. Perhaps the most vivid example of this litigation as a fight for justice comes from Howard. Here, he talks about his early thoughts about initiating litigation:

> This is not unlike *Braveheart*: There are so many beat-up crusty pieces of shit that live so close to the ground they have nothing to lose. And they've got torches lit and pitchforks aimed and they are going to come running down that hill ... because if [the Church] goes to court, and win[s], they are going to keep coming until one wins. And if [the Church] loses, it's going to prove that it can be beat and every other one is gonna stand in line doing what the one did before ... We know how to get dirty. We know how to be hungry, naked, without. We know how to take a beating, we know how to be hurt. We know how to suffer. It's our life. We're doing what we normally do! We're just bringing it with you! We're a bunch of good Catholic hens that have come home to roost!

These examples illustrate some of the frustration that survivors encountered in trying to make the Church bear witness to what it had done and failed to do and the consequences of its actions and omissions. In some sense, the stonewalling and minimizing denied the victims' very existences outright, not only as victims, but as members of the Church. By responding that way, the Church ultimately cut off these individuals, excluding them from Church support or comfort. For these victims, litigation became a way to force the Church back to the table, in essence, to make it "sit down and shut up."

Summary: Shifts in Awareness about the Abuse and the Church

Whatever the consequence, the establishment of truth was a critical piece in the early stages of litigation: survivors wanted the truth of the abuse, in its full extent, to be established so that both their personal and societal history could be accurately recorded. Filing litigation was a critical piece in that history. One survivor relayed an account where she told her story of childhood abuse to a reporter, and his response to her was that he would print the story "tomorrow" if she filed a lawsuit. In this sense, the litigation brought some legitimacy and gravitas to the survivors' claims.

In truth, it can be said that these initial pieces of the litigation in Boston absolutely worked in raising awareness, particularly in the United States. One of the survivors captures the tide shift toward the survivors:

> [In the beginning] my newspaper wrote an article and ... In the article he said that the first thing the Church needs to do is to stop paying these guys [survivors]. "They think they've won the pedophile lottery. How dare they come up and make accusations against good priests, let alone dead priests." Not only did he write that, he said that on the air. They played it over and over again. It became part of his commercial. This was *my* home newspaper ... Nothing bothered me more than when *my* home newspaper did that. Now, fast forward two years. The day after settlement. The editorial had said that what [some of the survivors did] was "prophetic." So was there a huge support from the Catholic community? At first, oh my God, no. They called us liars. We were called liars. Everyone said Joe X was crazy because he said the Cardinal knew. (Andrew)

Richard, an advocate, also captures this shift, but from his perspective as an attorney. In this narrative, he discusses how prior to 2002 he would be interviewed on local talk shows with hostility:

> I would go in and just take a beating and I did it because I wanted to understand what their point of view was and respond to it. And after the Attorney General's report in 2003, these people couldn't have been friendlier, and congratulatory and "What a wonderful job we did." I almost puked! But I also remember hearing people more on the street in places that I went to talking about, where there might have been comments before like, "Oh, they're fakers." That didn't come out anymore. It was: "This really happened."

The public discourse changed as a result of the litigation in Boston and the avalanche of documents secured through discovery. To no small extent, the truth about the Church and the abuse was established in short order in 2002.

---

[1] Portions of this material originally appeared in a somewhat different form in Balboni, Jennifer M. and Bishop, Donna M. 2010. "Transformative Justice: Survivor Perspectives on Clergy Sexual Abuse Litigation. *Contemporary Justice Review*, 13:133-154. Used by permission of the publisher.

[2] In these cases, only the plaintiffs' attorneys and the Church had access to names.

[3] This is a biblical reference: the Gospel of Matthew, Chapter 8, verse 16.

6

Anger, Disillusionment, and Hope

Nearly every litigant experienced hope and excitement at the start of the legal process; just the act of initiating the suit provided some sense of empowerment. In most cases, it also provided validation because survivors were believed (e.g., by their attorneys, family members, or the community, etc.). But the early period of excitement was followed by a long period of waiting; in most instances, suits were not settled for more than a year. During that time, many survivors forged significant relationships with each other and reassessed what they fought for. As more and more cases came to light, they became aware of the prevalence of abuse and the nature and magnitude of Church officials' efforts to shield it from public awareness. Many felt sickened by the toll of continuing victimization that was the price of diocesan strategies to silence victims and to geographically handle the problem of offending priests. Moved by these discoveries and supported by their fellow survivors, some began to push agendas for change within the Church and in larger social arenas. Others, struck by the scope of abuse and the missed opportunities to protect children from known child molesters, describe this period as one of disillusionment and, in some cases, despair. All of the survivors reported some strain, albeit to varying degrees, on their personal lives as a result of the litigation. These revelations helped shift the survivors' goals from what was initially fairly narrow to a much broader sense of mission and purpose.

Appalling Revelations

As legal scholar David Luban so aptly observed, the process of discovery in litigation is a "contact sport with an absentee umpire" (1995, p. 2648). Clergy sexual abuse cases are no exception to this rule. Post 2002, however, the process of discovery was not only disheartening in its adversariness, but also it produced an unusually prodigious set of documents about the extent of Church awareness concerning some of the sex offending priests. Their acquisition through legal discovery contributed to the evolution of the survivors' goals. Literally thousands of pages of previously classified documents were released and made public in the Boston and Springfield cases, offering the public a rare opportunity to understand both the scope of the problem and the Church's responses. Most survivors reported being horrified by the revelations contained in the formerly confidential documents:

> [When this started] I had no idea the magnitude of the abuse. (Connie)

> That's why I decided to file a lawsuit, because I figured, that is the only way to get access to these personnel records. So if the bishop was saying, "Well, we never had a problem with [this priest]," well, then they'd have to prove it. I found quite the opposite. I didn't expect that I would find something quite as powerful, and that so many bishops were in on it. (Lawrence)

These revelations involved revisiting the naming stage to come to a more global understanding of the problem of the abuse. Importantly, the realization that they were not alone, that others had been abused as well, prompted individual survivors to identify with the larger survivor group. The connections made proved to be very powerful.

Finding One's Brothers or Sisters

One of the more unique features of clergy sexual abuse litigation is the development of community. Nearly all of the survivors became connected to other survivors as a direct result of the litigation. In several cases, attorneys attempted to connect survivors for support and healing. Several advocates from different firms also tried to bring survivors together in hopes of building support networks (within legal constraints, of course). Believing such interaction was essential, one advocate even provided office space for survivor group meetings.

More often, however, networks were built on a web of informal relationships. In many cases, a survivor contacted a childhood friend whom he or she suspected might also have been abused by the same priest. The media also played an important role in this: survivors who had gone public became magnets for other survivors. One survivor talked about what happened to him after his name was published in a newspaper article about the litigation:

> What happened to me after that article—I couldn't take emails. I'd come home and there'd be, like, hundreds. It was getting ridiculous …

> They wanted to talk to me ... the first month my cell phone bill was
> $800! I didn't know what was going on ... I was literally on the phone
> all day long. (Fred)

Reporters also forged connections among survivors. Two survivors and
a few advocates reported instances in which reporters acted as
intermediaries for survivors:

> I got a call from a reporter, who said, "I got a call from someone who
> says he knows who you are and he wants to talk to you. He says he
> was your best friend." He told me who it was. He said, "He recognized
> who you were [even though his name was not identified in the
> article]." So he gave me his number and I called him and he had been
> abused by [the same priest] and he never told anybody, including his
> wife. He chose not to. (Henry)

These new relationships fostered a unique kind of defiant pride, and it
shaped the nature of the litigation. Fred captures this sentiment:

> It was like the "rebel rebel" in me had a reason now. [laughs] Now
> I've got a cause! I mean, I'm joking, but, it's like, the anger finally had
> a place to go. It was a big 360 [sic, 180]. It's amazing! Amazing. To
> me, in my life, that might be partly what God's doing.

This newly empowered critical mass—whether it be three
individuals offended against by the same priest, or the 500+ victims in
Boston—distinguishes clergy sexual abuse litigation from other types of
individual torts. Clergy sexual abuse litigation is a decidedly social
endeavor, characterized by collective awareness, mutual empathy, and
reinforcement for taking action. With the support of the larger group,
victims were able to take the shame they had passively borne for years
and transform it into a defiant action.

Goffman (1963) talks about managing "discreditable information"
through "group alignment." The development of "ego identity" involves
identifying with others who share similar histories. The survivors talk
passionately about meeting one another and the comfort they shared in
knowing they weren't the only ones who felt so ashamed about their
pasts:

> It was so nice to meet other people. It's like this big shaming secret
> that you think you're responsible for. And then your therapist tells you
> you're not responsible for it ... and you start kind of believing it. And
> you meet these other people. It's wonderful not to be alone in it.
> (Virginia)

It was good to be with people who understood how crazy we were getting. I mean, how difficult it was to intermingle your life with recovery, and how much we needed each other, to support each other. (Connie)

But relationship building was not always easy. Men especially acknowledged apprehension about being involved in a sexual abuse survivor group. In the following exchange, Fred reflects on his internal dialogue about being associated with the survivor community:

Fred: Men don't know how to acknowledge to another man [who has been sexually abused] ... It's so weird, it's so *weird* and I know it's not logical, but I would look at [another victim] and go, "Poor John. He got abused." Like he was—

JB: Different than you.

Fred: Yeah! ... I don't want nothing [sic] to do with these other victims! 'Cause to me, they have problems. I never said this to any of the guys, but I didn't want to be part of them. Why would I want to be part of this group, or movement?

Still, Fred overcame his uneasiness and developed several very strong relationships with other survivors. Similarly, Lewis talks about a significant transformation in the quality of his life after he connected with other men who had been abused by the same priest. He states:

It was the first time I could laugh and joke. I could walk into the room and say, "Holy shit! I'm not the only one. I went through that, too!" We would talk to each other about what happened. I felt comfortable for the first time.

Because of the context of this abuse—that it occurred with a "holy man," that it often involved same-sex relations, that the act was tinged with elements of religion—survivors took on inordinate self-blame and felt a profound sense of shame. Finding others who had struggled with the same shame helped survivors begin collectively to deflect responsibility for the abuse. Further, the survivor community became a safe space where individuals could feel accepted and cared about by others who had full knowledge of their pasts. Lewis states about his newfound brothers, "They are great. They are the most important people. [They] gave me a sense of security."

One advocate talks about the group dynamic of bringing several survivors together to talk about their cases:

[In the beginning of the litigation process] I saw people that kind of came and sat in the back and wouldn't say their names. By the end it was—I'm making up names—"John" and "Joe" and "Bill," and [they were] bringing wives and significant others, and people [were] hugging each other at the end. I think for a lot of people they were absolutely blown away to hear that John's story was *their* story, or Bill's story was *their* story. For people who had spent a lifetime thinking of themselves as screwed up, thinking of themselves as evil, of themselves as bad people, they finally started to understand that, in fact, it wasn't their fault. And I think a lot of that came from the process of talking to other people. That's not to say that it was successful for everybody, but for a lot of people, that commonality ... (Trevor)

Some of the connections survivors made were even closer to home. The litigation process prompted Douglas to reassess his own family relations. After learning that several members of his family had also been abused, Douglas began to understand his family better. He stated that those relationships had been strengthened as a consequence—albeit unintended—of the litigation. Two other survivors related how other members of their families also disclosed their own abuse—clergy and otherwise—at some point during the litigation process. Both were immeasurably grateful to have had the chance to rid themselves of the dark and shameful secrets that had separated them from their loved ones.

(Un)Happy Families

Curiously, "bands of brothers" (and sisters) often formed, sometimes around specific perpetrators. But just as suggested by the life histories of these survivors, these groups were hardly homogeneous or shared a singular purpose. Greta relays the diversity and sometimes fractious nature of the survivor community:

I'd hear other people say that they were representing survivors, and they'd say things and other people would say, "No, no, we don't feel that way." And I'd say, "Please just say 'I feel this way.''' Because we're different people. And we argue amongst ourselves. Like, for example, I was invited to [a Church function]. That was a big thing, who got invited and who didn't. I think it was the 'good survivors' vs. the 'angry survivors.' From the names I saw ... So I got a lot of hate mail—all from survivors ... And I understood why they were angry, of course, but it was misdirected ... Yes, there is this in-fighting ... I try to be reasonable and say, "I *understand* your anger." And [one survivor] would want us to spit [at members of the Church]. And I'd say, "You're the one who is going to get the attention, not the 50 of us here giving silent vigil." And he just said, "You're an idiot. Kiss my ass." And I'd say, [sweetly] "Let's just stop right here. This is not productive." But I understood his anger. Also, so many of them—myself included—are alcoholics, but were still drinking.

In particular, there were several infamous offenders whose victims' stories resonated and attracted dozens of other survivors who coalesced. Not all of the experiences with other survivors, however, were positive. Sadly, many survivors of lesser-known perpetrators felt estranged and isolated from these others:

> I always say: It's like each priest has a team. Like the [infamous priest] team has their own support group. And I'm on the [lesser known priest's] team and we have a terrible team. Our team doesn't want to play! All the people who won't come forward and stuff—and the people who came forward before—secretly and did secret settlements in the mid 1990s and stuff, most of them are quiet about it. ... I always think about it like we're at a cocktail party with all the victims. "Hi. I'm a [names his offender]." [gestures to walking up and meeting someone new:] "Well, nice to meet you, I'm a [another infamous priest]." At some point you feel like you're defined by your abuser.

Still, not all bonds were a result of abuse by a specific perpetrator, and survivors with different priest perpetrators did communicate. Two survivors also discussed particularly distressing—perhaps bordering on verbally abusive—interactions with other survivors that demonstrate how fractious the survivor community could be at times, particularly when survivors' litigation goals differed. In both cases, the survivors argued for a more conciliatory tack with the Church. Here, Isaac discusses how a survivor meeting turned against him when he tried to advocate for reconciliation and forgiveness:

> [Choosing his words carefully:] Each time I went [to a survivor meeting], I would find myself being frustrated, being angry, and as I shared some of my own victories, some of those people there—not all—but some people did not want to hear what I had to say, or were angry with me. ... They were not happy for me moving in a healthy direction. ... [Another victim] said to me, "What was it like [to receive an apology from the Bishop]?" I sat with him one on one. I said, "Do you know that you have to forgive these people? Do you know that part of this process is for you to resolve your bitterness toward the person that did this to you?" [His response was] "No way! No way in hell could [the priest or the bishop] ever go to heaven!"

Vincent talks about a similar reception from others when he tried to focus on survivor healing as opposed to compensation during settlement discussions. In this excerpt, he had just suggested that the group should negotiate longstanding counseling programs for survivors from the Church as part of the settlement:

> And [other survivors] are going, [mouth sounds of a flubbing bugle, heckling] "Shut up! You big baby! Whose side are you on?" I mean, they were cussing me out! I was like, whoa!

Still, most interactions with other survivors were positive in nature and effect. Rick, in particular, commented on significant relationships that had been forged as a result of the litigation process. The combination of the newly formed relationships, along with the information uncovered about the prevalence of abuse and the Church's attempts to silence victims, powerfully influenced a shift in survivors' goals.

Personal and Social Identities

Perhaps because the nature of this litigation is so personal, survivors often talked about how the litigation caused them to reflect upon their lives. Fred, for example, commented on his growing awareness of how the abuse had affected him:

> My motivation [at the beginning] was more for, "Let's just help the kids. Let's just stop this now. This is a good cause. I'm into it." And then as time went on, I had to realize, "Oh my God, I've got problems." And my problems come from this somewhat ...

Isaac talks about this as well:

> And I think I came to understand, through being involved in the legal process, that I deserved something financially, too. Because I was damaged. Had this not happened to me, I might have a great job today. I'm very talented. I'm talented in computers. I'm talented in electronics. Having the right mindset about myself may have produced greater ability for achievement. So that kind of settled in later, that, "You have robbed me of so much." And that was also in discussion, too. Because we were talking with other victims, etc. I was hearing all of these things and they were realizing as well, and came to the conclusion, "Hey, I'm in the same boat as you." And so, yes, the goals changed in that regard.

The litigation caused many survivors to reconsider not only their personal ego identities (Goffman 1963), but also their social identities. As such, not only were they coming to understand themselves better, but also many chose, or were forced, to deal with their new social status as a victim/survivor. For many, this meant dealing with serious tumult in their personal lives. During the course of litigation at least one survivor underwent a separation from his spouse, two reported high stress on their marriages and relationships with their children, four reported very strained relationships with their parents and siblings, at least two felt their careers had been hurt, and one reported a period of homelessness. However, the respondents in this study may have experienced less personal conflict than the group of litigants as a whole. Lydia's comments about personal strain for her clients were fairly typical for the advocates:

> But over time I think [the litigation] really wore on a lot of people. I don't think ... as much as we could have told them, "This is going to be a long process, it could be years and years," I don't think any of them really understood that, and understood how hard you were going to have to fight. So there were a lot of divorces, deaths, attempted suicides, people that just went through all kinds of ups and downs in their personal lives during this process.

Lydia's comments note an exceptionally important facet of this type of litigation: it dredged up ghosts of the past, forcing survivors to confront horrors that they rarely had spoken of previously[1]. Waking these sleeping dogs necessitated renegotiation of their personal and social identities. In short, the litigation triggered a certain amount of trauma for the survivors. Although some would eventually report stronger marriages or stronger familial ties as an end result—as most of the survivors in this study did—, the process involved a certain amount of bloodletting before that point would come.

Throughout the course of the litigation, these developments—strains on personal relationships, horrifying revelations through legal discovery, newfound relationships with peers—shaped the meaning of litigation for survivors. Eventually, litigation became a sidebar to other things in their lives, including advocacy work related to preventing childhood sexual abuse.

Evolving Meaning and Higher Purposes

During the period between initiation of litigation and settlement, survivors relayed a variety of goals, including getting at the real truth (e.g., the discovery of even more victims), vengeance, monetary compensation, prevention, and raising awareness. Andrew speaks about the changes he went through with regard to goals:

> Andrew: And as those [reports of abuse] started coming out through one or two pages of files, I started learning more, things started to build upon themselves. Then it was just unbelievable. And I was bullshit.

> JB: I'm trying to sense if your goals changed.

> Andrew: Yes, over the last two years, they went through a whole range of things. Never knowing—never ever fathoming—what the truth was. At that point [in the beginning] we're talking about two or three priests. Two or three guys. And then it started unfolding. I was like, "God, we need systemic change. We gotta change the laws in the state because we can't prosecute these people." Then when [a close member of his family] came out [and also disclosed abuse], it suddenly became about protecting my [child]. It's been an ever evolving last two years. There was no game plan. I had no idea what I was doing. No idea …You know, I was not thinking long-term goals. Not because I just couldn't see that far. It was all: What can we do this week? What can we do next week? What can we do next month? What can we do the following month? It was—get out there, tell the truth. Meet with [the representatives of the Church]. Get the church to do something. Get them into programs. Get them to agree to do things. Get [members of the Church] to meet the parents. We were actually running *blind*. I mean, there was nothing out there. There was no help for anyone coming at that point.

> JB: So initially you're responding to silence, then you're out there reacting to bits of information.

> Andrew: It was the "Oh my God" theory. "Oh my God: The files are coming out." "Oh my God: There's [dozens of] men [involved with this particular priest]." Wives, ex-wives, kids, mothers, fathers are now saying, "Oh my God: That's why!" The only people who weren't saying "Oh my God" was the Church.

> JB: Because they knew.

Andrew: Right. So it was long-term goals—never had. It was all short term. The very simple things of trying to get a phone call [from the Church]. It was the very basic teaching these people how to treat people like human beings: [To the Church] Return my phone call!

Later, he tries to summarize the complexity of the litigation goals:

It was much more simple. It was about right and wrong. It was about good overcoming evil, and if you don't believe in that then [trails off] ... then what's the point of living? I mean, I never ... hindsight? Truth be told: It was about bringing them to the table. Make them accountable. They have a responsibility to change the future for our kids. I mean, that's what my goals were knowingly or unknowingly. That's really [it]. Tell the truth! Be accountable! You have a responsibility here.

George also talks about how his goals shifted through the course of litigation:

... after [the Church] cut me off [refused to acknowledge his letters or to pay for counseling], I mean, I wanted revenge. I can tell you that at different times, my motives changed, my sense of justice changed, and keeping my eyes on my motives and stuff. Early on, it was "I want revenge." Early on, it was "I want to survive. I need money to survive." After that, there were moments of, "I want to be part of a change. I want to be part of changing something, of creating something that can be helpful, that can be healing, to bring some reconciliation." In other moments, it was pure money. I'm not going to lie to you. "I want as much money as I can get." In some moments, there were multiple motives. I'm certainly not going to say that my motives [were] idealist or altruistic all along, because they are not. It's mostly mixed motives ... My sense of justice changed, I've had different thoughts on justice from not thinking there is any justice at all to justice being, "I hope the Catholic Church in the U.S. closes its doors," to justice would be for me as an individual doing enough inner work or healing work where I'm not passing the same guilt, fears, neuroses to the next generation.

Revenge, however, usually proved to be only a transient motivation. Douglas' comments were very much in the minority:

Douglas: Oh, and I want to say something right now [adamantly]: The Catholic Church is my *sworn enemy! Utterly!* I just—there is no word for the amount of anger I have—I'm working through it. The Catholic Church is paying for my anti-depressants. They are still paying for my counseling. But I'll be fucking damned if I spend any of the money they gave me—

JB: On therapy or anything like that.

Douglas: Exactly.

JB: What were your goals?

Douglas: To do as much damage, verbally, as I possibly can to the Catholic Church.

Most survivors, however, relayed a confluence of shifting goals, more in line with George's thoughts. The common thread through the survivor comments about later goals was the idea that litigation could not achieve their goals. Instead, survivors began to focus on other means to achieve the ends they sought, and the litigation became secondary to bigger issues in their lives.

In general, those who were well-connected within the survivor community frequently channeled their energies into advocacy, believing that change could come about if enough political pressure could be brought upon the Church. Many survivors worked to change statutes of limitations or charitable immunity laws. Others—usually those who had made fewer connections (e.g., Douglas or Matthew)—became disillusioned entirely, believing that substantive change could not be achieved. In either case, as the litigation wore on, fewer and fewer people believed that litigation could achieve a desirable goal. In the following exchange, Christopher relays the feeling that the litigation became a sidebar to his advocacy work:

JB: As the litigation went on, did your goals change?

Christopher: I gave up. I mean, I said, "Ok, whatever you guys [lawyers] do—settle—fine." I didn't see that that was the way to obtain my goals. ... [My goal was] to fight it on a different level ...

JB: So what happened to your goals? Were there new goals?

Christopher: To fight it on a different level, including standing out alone in front of the chancery. [speaking somewhat ironically:] Including starting this nonprofit with the money that I will be getting from them! That will also deal with clergy abuse, but all abuse. I just want to create a safe place. And I also want to be an activist about this stuff. The goals have shifted. There was, and still is, plenty of anger and revenge. But it's just getting me nowhere. So I have to find a better way to come to grips with this.

Psychologist Judith Herman talks about "finding a survivor mission" as a final stage of healing for child victims of sexual abuse. "These survivors recognize a political or religious dimension in their misfortune and discover that they can transform the meaning of their personal tragedy by making it the basis for social action" (1997, p. 207). Two survivors describe how advocacy work has helped them to turn trauma into triumph:

> One thing I'd love to say is that the last couple of years, being out there and working for this better world—I don't know what you'd call it—has been the most meaningful time in my life. It's been a roller coaster. A lot of work and a lot of sleepless nights. But I wouldn't change it for a second. I'd do it all again. (Beth)

> [This litigation] is life-defining, but only because I followed up. If I had left it at [the settlement] it would have been killing. If I had left it at litigation and didn't get the apology and admission of guilt ... I have to say, what's even more important is if we get legislation. It's much more important than my personal lawsuit. What's more important is to get external forces involved. Not a personal injury lawyer, but the justice system. So, because in my own little world, yes, I got it together, I have a house, da da da [sic] ... But if that's all I did was get this house, my life would be meaningless. It's about doing something that is larger than your own small world. (Elise)

Recognizing the power of advocacy work to both heal within and help others, Dr. Herman states, "Social action offers the survivor a source of power that draws upon her own initiative, energy, and resourcefulness but that magnifies these qualities far beyond her own capacities. It offers her an alliance with others based on cooperation and shared purpose" (1997, p. 207).

In many cases, activism went beyond clergy sexual abuse to take account of the broader social context that facilitated its occurrence. For several survivors, abuses of power and human rights were the primary issues with which they identified:

> Really, I didn't want [the litigation to end]. I wanted to continue hammering away at these points about power. I mean, my focus on this has been the abuse of power, not sex. And I think because the sexual component of what happened to me was less than for a lot of people, what I realized was that the betrayal ... The harm was caused at the

first kiss, not anything subsequent to that. It was the betrayal that did me in. It was the abuse of the power and not the sex. (Henry)

I'd like to think that there are greater implications [from the litigation] than just for preventing sexual abuse by priests ... I hope it's contributed to better attitudes overall by how people treat other people. I'm thinking now of parents who beat their children. It's wrong. It doesn't do anything. It's humiliating. It's shameful. I'd like to think that society is evolved and is becoming better. (Matthew)

Because I see it as such a larger problem than the Church. The Church becomes a vehicle. [We] are working on the legislation, repealing the statute of limitations. I truly would like to see this culture more respectful of children and continue to break the silence. One of the things that is different about [this situation than] the 1980s [revelations of sexual abuse] is that it is actually an institution that you can address. It has overtly and covertly supported the abuse ... [I'm trying to] bring to consciousness about the abuse of children in this country. And the abuse of power. It's not just the abuse of children. I mean, that's what gets people. But the way power is abused, whether it's through racism or sexism or homophobia, or whether it's through religion, it's just outrageous. (Anna)

Conclusions

These survivors relayed how the goals of litigation shifted for them in response to information uncovered through legal discovery and newly formed relationships with other survivors, facilitated through the litigation process and the media involvement. Many survivors described a transformation in their identities. For many, litigation was relegated to a position of secondary importance as survivors came to understand that they couldn't sue their way to either personal healing or social reform. Some took their energy and put it to work in advocacy projects, while others became disillusioned. The role of the attorney-client relationship was a critical piece in these transformations.

---

[1] For a discussion about the benefits and harm of disclosure, see (McNulty and Wardle 1994) and (Sauzier 1989).

7
The Attorney-Client Relationship

This guy [had been in the military]. He was one of the people, I remember him specifically because he was living in a veterans' homeless shelter at the time that we first met. And, um, again, [he had] some severe problems he had gone through. I remember [this decorated military man] just crying and crying and crying after [he told me his history of abuse and relational problems and] I said, "That makes you normal." You could just feel that air get sucked out of the room as he started to cry. And at the end of the process [litigation], he said, "I have something for you and it's going to blow you away." I didn't think much of it. He called and said he wanted to come in and, he came in, and presented to us, me [and some of the staff], his gold star, his two bronze stars and his [other medals]. He said, "I've been in the fight of my life and you were my soldier in that fight. You're having these means more to me than my having these." (Daniel, a clergy sexual abuse attorney)

To say that the attorneys' role in clergy sexual abuse litigation is complicated would be an enormous understatement. Survivors never felt apathetic about their attorneys: the nature of this litigation is intense, and as a result, the attorney-client relationship reflects that intensity. While the quote from Daniel discusses the heroic role that many played, this is just one of many roles that the advocates played: from knights in a pitched battle, to social workers tirelessly listening to their clients' histories, to mercenaries fighting for profit. On some level, all of the survivors felt loyalty to their attorneys for taking their cases at all; many felt their attorneys were the only people who initially believed their stories and who did not judge them as spoiled individuals. But initial feelings of gratitude usually gave way to questions about attorney motivations and sensitivities. Legal strategy needed to reconcile survivor needs with civil remedies, and as will be discussed, it sometimes made for an odd coupling.

Gratitude and Disenchantment

Knights

Most survivors expressed a strong sense of gratitude that their attorneys had believed in them enough to take their cases. Clients reciprocated by placing a high level of trust and confidence in their attorneys. As the opening story in this chapter illustrates, attorneys frequently were portrayed as champions who had aligned with survivors to fight for them. Andrew communicates the weight of the expectations he placed on his attorney:

> I told [my lawyer] when I first met him, "I'm putting my life in your hands. That doesn't come easy. Don't let me down."

Some attorneys appreciated, on some level, the power the litigation could have for certain clients. One lawyer relays the story of one man's empowerment, which she witnessed as a product of the litigation:

> I remember one specific person, when they announced the settlement, for the first time he stood in front of the camera and said [forcefully:], "My name is John Smith and I am a victim of Father X." And he did it! And for him to go out publicly was a *huge* change. And at that moment, it came to me, the phrase … "recalled to life." … And these guys [like the characters from *A Tale of Two Cities*], I really felt that they were liberated, they had reclaimed their lives. They were doing something themselves—*through us as their agents*—but they were taking control back. To me, that was the most powerful, rewarding, and exhilarating thing …

In these instances, both the attorneys and the clients realized the potential for this type of litigation.

Early in the litigation, survivors generally were pleased with the quality of representation, particularly when some of the attorneys engaged in very public media warfare. Not only did the attorneys believe their clients, but also they were willing to put their own reputations on the line for them. Particularly in litigation from 2002 forward, attorney strategies met with great success: the initial goal of establishing truth was advanced, at least to some degree, by the mere filing of the lawsuit. This came through media reports of survivor claims and the groundswell of support for survivors that sprang up from a variety of community groups (e.g., VOTF, SNAP, the LINKUP, Speak Truth To Power). It was clear that survivors felt deep appreciation for the work their advocates did, particularly at the outset of the litigation, when their primary goal was to listen to these survivors and provide an initial accounting of their history.

Interestingly, even when survivors were disappointed with the legal process or frustrated with what they perceived to be procedural injustices along the way, most did not blame their attorneys. Notably, many survivors were sensitive to, but willing to forgive, perceived slights by their attorneys. For example, one survivor reported that he was not angry when calls to his attorney were rarely returned:

> I don't fault [the lawyers] for it. They have how many hundreds of cases they deal with? They've got to deal with what they've got to deal with. Obviously the guy that was raped on a daily basis for two years straight gets more attention. I was only molested for about a year. (Matthew)

Greta reported at least one instance of arguably unethical behavior on the part of her attorney, when he invited the media to a private and confidential meeting without her permission. Still, she insisted that he "meant well," apologetically offering that, "Anyway, he's a character."

Social Workers

All of the attorneys recognized that listening to their clients performed an important, even transformative, service, particularly at the outset of the litigation when a primary goal for clients was to be believed. Beyond this initial point in litigation, some advocates continued listening, holding what only can be described as quasi-therapy sessions. One advocate discusses her take:

> There were some clients I talked to every day. Every day! One guy used to call me daily, and say, "Send your bill to the Archdiocese. I get more from talking to you than I do from their therapist." I mean, he was a very needy guy, obviously. But, [he] just needed to check in, you know, and feel like somebody cared about him.

Many advocates relayed stories of talking to some clients for hours on the phone, and not necessarily about legal strategy. Amy relays how she wanted to play a semi-therapeutic role with her clients:

> I felt like I really didn't want to lose the connection and the control, basically. It felt like we could *handle* their calls. Of course, it was not the same as a therapist, especially when they had a therapist. Or, some

people just refused to see a therapist, so we had to be there. There was no one else that they would talk to but us.

While some advocates were happy to provide a shoulder to lean on, several advocates noted that they weren't trained to do that job, and that what many of their clients needed was a professional therapist. Nearly all of the advocates understood that the litigation could have the net personal effect of waving a stick inside a hornet's nest for these clients: hospitalizations, divorces, break-ups, and other life crises were not uncommon in these cases. Several advocates candidly spoke about their fears that a client would become homicidal or suicidal. But as Janet's and Amy's narratives suggest, the emotional pull for the advocates was very powerful, although this pull was dealt with very differently by different firms. On the more organized end, some offices had full-time, on-call social workers and well-established relationships with active survivor advocate groups. In these situations, one or more social workers were part of the legal office staff. Here, one advocate talks about the importance of having a social worker on staff:

> It added a dimension in terms of what we could do. I mean, most of the people didn't want to talk to the lawyers. They wanted to talk to [the social worker]. I mean, they wanted to know what was going on with their case, but when it was two in the morning, if they had a problem, it was [the social worker] that they called. And it was [the social worker] that answered those calls.

In addition to the staff social worker, one office employed attorneys with social service or psychology backgrounds to bring a greater level of sensitivity to their clients. In addition, feeling that connection to other survivors is integral to healing, attorneys in this office also had other victims "on call" to talk with clients. Several attorneys saw peer referral—voluntary, of course—as part of their job: to connect people with others who share similar backgrounds. One attorney comments on the importance of these connections within his practice:

> In order to heal, survivors need to come to understand that the shame they carried, the guilt they carried, they were not to blame. The confusion and the guilt are common. With others, they learn that they are not alone, it's not their fault. They can't learn that on their own. This is a necessary and integral resource for reclaiming power. (Jason)

One of the smaller offices maintained professional relationships with specific providers who served as ad hoc consultants for the practice: not on the official payroll, but in close contact because of the large numbers of clients in common. In this particular case, the attorneys felt that the providers were part of the team.

Other offices employed quasi-referral services where paralegals would make connections for the clients. Finally, the least organized system involved offering triage referrals: when a client called in crisis, the attorney would help provide a referral.

The relevance of social work in these cases cannot be underscored, and the more sensitive advocates understood that these types of cases required more than legal strategy—whether it be through a social worker on staff or a formalized referral system. Lydia, an advocate, describes the dual role of providing legal services while tending to social work concerns:

> But I always think I had this goal of being both sympathetic to them, trying to be an understanding ear, at the same time educating them on the law. "I understand this happened to you and how horrible this was for you, but I am constrained by what I'm allowed to do *by law,* and the arguments that I can make—and I'm going to be creative—and try and do the best that I can, but there are some hurdles that we may not be able to get over with this." A lot of times I felt like I was the only one with that voice. ... "But let's do something to help make this process easier for you." And try to get them involved in support groups. Try to get them to see a therapist on a regular basis. Try to get them to understand how the legal field and what they went through have to mix in this arena. Because I'm not a therapist. And that's not what I was hired to do.

It must be noted that the attorneys and other legal advocates spoke with strong emotion when discussing their clients. Rare was the advocate who spoke plainly about legal strategy without discussing the human impact. These strong emotions varied, however. One advocate wept over the "wreckage of lives" that the abuse had caused; some very nearly spit nails when discussing the Church's role in the abuse; others became ardent advocates for different legislative reforms; and still others brimmed with pride over clients they came to think of as "their own children" who had faced down their demons and prevailed. It was very clear that—whatever referral systems were in place—the attorneys were invested in these cases, both professionally and emotionally. One advocate talks about her personal goals in working with clergy sexual abuse victims:

> There is a part of me that—I like that—I like being indignant. But it fueled me, and I felt a real personal mission with our clients. I felt like I was enabling them to do something that I could never have done [for victims in her own family] … To me, it transcended history to be able to give that chance to others. (Justine)

The emotional pull was strong in these cases for virtually all of the attorneys.

Hired Hands and Other Mercenaries

Although victories had been won in early stages of litigation, the gamesmanship of the litigation caused many to reassess both whether their attorneys understood the meaning of this litigation for survivors, as well as why their attorneys had become involved in the cases in the first place. This brought on various epiphanies about the attorneys' limitations and about the nature and general potential for civil remedies overall. Even when survivors felt positively about their attorneys, which was often, they noted how interactions with them disabused them of the notion that the attorneys truly understood the nature of their cases and the trauma involved. In the following quotes, Joshua and Henry talk about attorneys involved in these cases:

> I think they are well-intentioned, but they don't get it. They do not get it. They do not understand the nuances and the implications of the little pieces, the emotional pieces. And it's not their job. It's not what they're doing, that's not why we hired them. (Joshua)

> The lawyers are not social workers. They do their job. They have no consideration for emotional content. That's been my experience. If there is any expectation of getting any kind of emotional resolve out of the legal process, forget it. If anything, it has been traumatizing to deal with the lawyers. (Henry)

Similarly, Christopher talks about his attorney's insistence to move forward toward settlement with no perceived consideration of his emotional state, and he would remind him that he needed time to think over proposals, replying sardonically, "Safety first. There are obviously triggers here," adding, "You're supposed to have a social worker [on staff]. Why don't you talk to her? She'll clue you in."

In the following interaction, Joshua makes a similar mental indication about the nature of litigation as he describes a small altercation between his attorney and him where the attorney misquoted him in an affidavit, and Joshua expressed his frustration that his attorney had cited the facts of his claims incorrectly:

> He basically totally withdrew from me from what had been, on some level, almost a peer relationship. It became totally, "Don't you think for a minute that we're equals and that you can talk to me that way." … I think [the attorneys] are well intentioned, but they don't get it. … *But,* there are some really important things for people to know, if you're looking for that from an attorney, you're going to be heartbroken. (Joshua)

The key piece here is that Joshua's truth—the nature of the abuse and the case itself—were not being adequately represented by his attorney, which infuriated him. When he revealed his frustration to the attorney, the attorney rebuffed him, indicating the hierarchy of their relationship and minimizing the importance of that truth.

Several of the survivors talked about how they didn't feel like their attorneys understood what was truly at stake for them in the litigation. After being yelled at by her attorneys for being too pleasant to the Church attorneys, Connie talks about her realization about the nature of litigation:

> The lawyers I had were all really good. But I'm very good about setting my boundaries, and saying, "I can't do this." They pushed me a lot. That day that [my attorney] yelled at me … during the deposition, that was really hard for me. I'm thinking, "You have no idea how hard this is for me." But he was right. They have to look at it as this whole different side. And it's not ever about justice, it never seems. It's about—I don't think the legal system is about justice. I'm sorry! [laughs]

In that interaction, she mentally links the negative interaction with her changing views about litigation and its potential for justice. It should be noted, however, that Connie's first comment was positive about her attorneys. Elise has similar feelings:

> My lawyer: I actually even like him. He's a very entertaining person. And he's very … [trailing off, laughs] and even though I was deceived, I wouldn't say that he deceived me. It was more like—he was doing his thing as a lawyer.

Most survivors shared that evaluation: they liked and appreciated their attorneys, despite feeling like justice was out of reach in the current litigation system.

Greta echoes this theme as she notes how a subtle interaction with her attorney after she finished her arbitration left her feeling like the attorney didn't understand the meaning of litigation for her:

> When it was over—my hearing—the judge left the room, and everyone left except [my attorney] and the other lawyer, and he kept saying, "That was powerful. You were great. That was powerful." And that really hit me the wrong way, because I wasn't performing. To me, it was gut-wrenching. I said to my brother, "I'm just holding on here."

Although she knew he was trying to be supportive, Greta felt that the attorney's comment missed the gravity of what had transpired in the arbitration for her.

Another survivor reports that, because of time pressures, attorneys frequently failed to explain procedural rights and rules:

> Liam: These civil lawsuits, first of all, should be explained to clients, because they don't even understand the dynamics of the lawsuit itself!
>
> JB: You don't think the lawyers explained it?
>
> Liam: Not at all. Never did. Not well. And I'm an articulate guy, I'm a guy that can read between the lines, I'm a guy that tried to read about it. I was still confused. Didn't know what the parameters of my rights were. Didn't know what I could ask for, didn't know that I had a right, that they weren't being represented—I was having them represent me ... But don't be Joan of Arc when you're really a hired gunslinger!

As noted in Liam's narrative, many began to question the attorney's financial motivations. Christopher also raises suspicions about the attorney's financial motivations in the following passage:

> I know more victims than they do, which was frustrating, because when I would say that, they would ask, "Can I have his number?" That kind of crap. And I'd say, "That's not why I'm sharing this with you." That was another reason why I [told my attorney] to end the litigation ... They need to make money for whoever they are answering to. And then they could sue for [the other people]. I mean, they didn't say this, but it's fairly transparent. (Christopher)

He goes on to question those motives more directly:

> I mean, how many times do you sue the diocese over the same priest, knowing the priest is still out there? That's just not right. So [the

attorney is] filling his pockets, making money and creating more clients, virtually.

By the end of the litigation, many survivors had come to view their attorneys as a type of mercenary. In the following passage, Liam discusses this with more than a little scorn:

> The question was, "Litigation: would I do it again?" I don't know if I'd do it again. It didn't solve anything. It gave me a paycheck! The rest of it I was going to be doing anyway. It was a waste of money. It was a waste of my time! And somebody told me that when I settled this lawsuit I could get on with my healing. Are you out of your mind? And it did—it put a complete stop on everything that we were doing. We fought this lily pad to lily pad, story to story, day to day in the court. We were fighting the wrong issues. And our lawyers thought they were helping us. They are gunslingers, man. They are hired guns to get money. They are nothing else.

Despite this disillusionment, survivors rarely spoke contemptuously about their attorneys, and when they did, they usually would balance negative statements with other more positive ones:

> I was outraged at [this attorney] ... I thought that [his conduct in the media] was unethical and immoral. Outrageous, the behavior of that lawyer in particular! But, it's like, I'm grateful for all the work the lawyers have done ... (Anna)

They may have been disappointed, even angry in some cases, but there was always a trace of gratitude in their expressions about the attorneys. This mix of gratitude and disenchantment may be the emblem for such relationships. Their feelings about their attorneys mirrored their feelings about the litigation in general: grateful at the start, disillusioned by the end.

Legal Strategy and Collective Representation

One area of concern for both litigants and attorneys was the complexity of consolidated mass torts. Technically, the bundling of cases does not qualify as a formal class action, but it functions very much like one in pragmatic terms: the attorneys strategize and litigate based upon the entire lot of clients, and less on behalf of particular individuals. Collective representation differs from class action suits, which have the advantages of having formalized judicial oversight for specific processes in the litigation. Judges supervise class action attorneys to make sure they are providing legal services for the entire class, and negotiations tend to be better organized with judicial oversight. The needs of the class are made explicitly clear to clients at the outset, as opposed to collective representation, where informed consent can be more variable.

These types of cases are complex, in that they involve a double-edged sword. Legal scholar Howard Erichson (2003) explains:

> Such collective representation is not necessarily a bad thing. To the contrary, effective litigation sometimes requires it. Collective representation enables clients to pursue litigation that otherwise would present insurmountable obstacles. But outside of class actions, the profession's failure to recognize the collective nature of much litigation has left clients unprotected, and has engendered an ethical murkiness that leaves lawyers unsure whether they owe their loyalty to the individual or to the collective (p. 2).

Because of the lack of clear formalized protocols, the individual client may feel disappointed, as Fred points out in the following passage:

> And they had a whole bunch of people to worry about, not just me. What I'm saying is, it's correct what they did, but the good of the many sometimes loses the personalities and personal touch that you need in this.

Here, a different survivor discusses the unintended consequence of competition among victims that consolidated mass torts engender:

> Because as far as I knew I was the only one with that particular priest at [this firm]. It made me feel weak again because what happened to me wasn't that big a deal compared to everything else. It really screws you up. (Matthew)

In terms of attorney-client communication, one attorney admitted to using the media as a way to communicate developments to his clients, as individual phone calls would have been time-consuming. While this strategy was probably more efficient, it may have caused some clients to feel left out.

Roberta, an advocate, talks about another potentially damaging dynamic to individual clients involved in collective representation:

> I think in some of the law firms, some people got more attention than others did when they were represented by the same lawyers. And that gets very dicey. It's like, in a family, the favorite child, jockeying for

[position or privilege] ... Then you have the dynamic of survivor against survivor.

Jeff talks about an incident in which he felt that his client needs were being subjugated to others' goals. He remembers clearly articulating to his attorneys that, "This is not 500 men's firm. This is *my* firm right now. This is my life."

Even the advocates recognized that consolidated mass torts had particular nuances and pitfalls. In the following passage, one advocate reflects on the issues involved in representing so many clients:

> I could probably think back to situations that I would have handled differently, but overall, I think I tried to really stay in my role as their advocate who is constrained by certain things. I mean, I was constrained by what [the] policy was and strategy was on the whole. We had to keep that in mind. We were not just representing this one person, we were representing a very large group and we had to make decisions very carefully based on what was for the greatest good. (Trevor)

Trevor goes on to talk about the risks of representing so many clients:

> We were also cognizant that we were on very dangerous ground—this was the Catholic Church. If we made one mistake, it could jeopardize everybody. So we wanted to be very careful to the group as a whole ...

In terms of the benefits of such suits, many attorneys noted that they were aware that significant collective representation (e.g., the clergy sexual abuse litigation) had the potential to change societal perceptions, to shape legislation, and to change institutional policies. One attorney talked about the potential for these collective cases to change policies within the Catholic Church, analogizing it to helping turn a "supertanker." Others commented on the societal shift in perceptions that occurred when the litigation exploded, and how the bias shifted from blaming the victim to placing the blame on the Church. Several attorneys were intimately involved in drafting legislation to extend the statute of limitations for victims of sexual abuse, a topic that undoubtedly had ripened in different communities in society as a product of the mass litigation. Several attorneys took pride in having been part of these positive changes.

Without question, collective representation suits present advantages in terms of negotiating power, but lawyers also have challenges in terms of being able to adequately represent or communicate to the individual client.

On Justice in the Civil System

Perhaps most importantly, interactions with the attorneys facilitated survivors understanding the limitations of civil remedies. Perhaps one of the most robust findings in this research is the overall mismatch between legal advocate and survivor goals. Fred cogently sums this up: "But it wasn't just about money [for us], but for [the lawyers] it was, because that's their job." Survivors, in most cases, were looking for things outside of money, things typically not found within the traditional tort system. On the other hand, while the personal injury attorneys often recognized that survivors sought a different type of justice, they usually felt constrained to work within the traditional tort model.

Lawyers generally talked about money as the best way to achieve justice. Trevor and Janet, respectively, equate the value of money in place of more noble goals:

> They wanted an acknowledgement of the betrayal. And that's where the money came in. It was too late for simply "I'm sorry." It needed to hurt the Church somehow. I don't mean that in the sense of a sadistic desire to … but they wanted the Church to understand that, "You know what? You've got to give up something because you caused me to give up something." There needed to be a little equity in the process. The money became a symbol for that. And so I think they wanted some meaningful acknowledgement that the Church did them wrong. (Trevor)

> Janet: Yeah. People say to you, "It's not about the money." Well, we've heard that for 25 years. Well, this *is* about the money, for the most part. [laughs] It is! A civil case is not going to put anybody behind bars with these cases. We would love to! I mean, I would love to castrate most of these [perpetrators]. But it's not going to happen through this venue. So it is about the money. And for them, it's about the [Church] acknowledging that something was awry and that they dropped the ball. And that ball is going to cost them. And that's how they felt. Whether it was the $80k or the $300k, that's where they were all coming from.

> JB: The money was an acknowledgement.

> Janet: That's right.

The calculus of "more money, more justice" was the yardstick they held out to determine equity. When asked about the overall fairness of one settlement, one attorney replied:

> No, I don't [think it was fair]. I think it was inconsequential in terms of what the Church could have afforded to pay. I think there was a lot of unfairness in the process … I think the amount they paid is miniscule compared to the amount of damage done to these individuals. With the level of proof we had on gross negligence of the individuals … [the Church] knew the stuff was going on—the amount was a pittance. (Will)

Another advocate echoed this theme when asked about the fairness of the settlement:

> What is fair? No, I don't think it was fair. Of course not. The survivors didn't get nearly enough for what they'd been through. No one was going to get rich from this settlement. Some got money toward the first down payment for their first house. (Walter)

He added that, in other parts of the country, similar cases have yielded significantly more money; while his clients were capped at $300 thousand, similar cases in other parts of the country were yielding $2 million to $5 million each. Here, another advocate talks about feeling forced to deal in terms of money:

> Well, the Church has a language that partially is in terms of dollars and cents. And that's the way they spoke.

While most of the attorneys focused on the dollar figure as an end to itself, several also noted that forcing the Church to pay might also bring about reform:

> [By suing] the victim will make people do the right thing because in the long run, it's cheaper. By doing this [litigation] repeatedly, [the Church] has been clubbed in the head enough to learn.

Several of the survivors agreed with this cynical assessment:

> You know, it's not the overwhelming number of people reporting it that is making change, it's the money. Because they knew for a long time and it really didn't … [trails off]. This stuff—they aren't surprised by what's come forward—most of this stuff they knew about

already. So, um, it's not doing the right thing on their part that is their motivation—it's protecting themselves. (Francis)

However, it must be noted that survivors were discouraged deeply by the idea that the money was the only language the Church understood.

These tendencies to focus on the monetary outcome demonstrate the gap in ideology between attorneys and their clients. Most attorneys I spoke with focused on the monetary amount of settlement; most survivors I spoke with talked about more lofty justice goals. When they did talk about the money, it was usually to observe contemptuously that it was the only language to which the Church would listen.

Almost every survivor I talked to sued not because they primarily wanted monetary damages. Survivors had other goals in mind: establishing truth about the past and the Church, implementing prevention strategies so that others would not be similarly abused, rooting out corruption within the Church, raising awareness about child abuse or the abuse of power, or letting other victims know they were not alone. Vincent's goals are fairly typical:

> The lawyer said to me, "What do you want out of this lawsuit?" I said, "I want three things … You hear people talk about the money. Money don't mean shit to me. [sic] I'm a recovering alcoholic. I don't smoke; I don't drink … I don't need a friggin' dime. But I want this priest removed, and I want an apology acknowledging that I was raped as a boy and that they are sorry. I want acknowledgement about what was done to me. I don't want "alleged" in front of my name. I don't want to be a survivor. I want to be a human being who was assaulted as a boy."

The survivors often felt ambivalent about the money. Worse, a few felt that they had prostituted themselves for it. Many legal advocates understood that money alone was not enough, but still felt it was their primary goal in the litigation. The notable exception to this was the one legal advocate who had implemented quasi-restorative processes in order to give some control back to the victims. He saw litigation as, first and foremost, a strategy to regain power for the victims:

> They reclaim the power that was robbed from them, by filing suit. This confronts the perpetrator and his supervisor. This action is affirmation that they are believed. (Jason)

This particular firm tried to make the process very victim-centered and, when possible, worked collaboratively with the Church to assist the victim in healing. This might involve confronting the perpetrator or his supervisor, asking for an apology or a meeting, setting up programming, or opening up different options that the victim initiates. One major goal of settlement, according to this advocate, is to "tell his or her story in their own words and articulate their needs from the Church and express their pain." Once these needs were addressed, only then were economic goals discussed.

Lastly, only a few survivors felt badly about accepting monetary compensation once they received the settlement; most saw it as a tangential issue. The money had to act as a proxy for the justice that most survivors desired.

Summary

Survivors clung to whatever justice agent they could to achieve some element of fairness. Despite good intentions on all sides, the result may have been somewhat of a mismatch, with survivors trying to achieve a higher purpose than traditional settlements typically demonstrate. Negotiations and settlement processes brought these goals into even sharper focus.

8

The End Game: The Good, The Bad, and the Really Ugly

When you blind a child, there is no system in the world who can bring back his sight. (Howard)

Closure in clergy sexual abuse cases, whether it be the Boston Global Settlement, the Springfield settlement, or other cases, usually was experienced as arduous and protracted by the survivors. Bringing these cases to an end involved revisiting the original goals, coming to a resolution about viable options, perhaps celebrating some victories, but always mourning what was lost—both legally and emotionally. This final stage of disputing brought further meaning to this journey in survivors' lives.

Most of the survivors I spoke with went through an arbitration process. This section will focus primarily on those who went through the Boston and Springfield settlement processes. In these cases, once the Church accepted the litigants' affidavits as true, the arbitration process was not adversarial in nature. An independent consulting firm was contracted to provide this service, with one arbitrator present alongside the survivor, their attorney, and any other witnesses. Many survivors were invited to bring pictures. Sessions lasted approximately two hours, and varied in tone depending on the attorney, who set the format.

Survivors and their advocates ascribed a great deal of meaning to the arbitration process—some of it good, some bad, and some really ugly. The good involved being able to tell one's story to an unbiased listener, and in doing so, revisiting and sometimes exorcising the ghosts of the past. The bad, however, involved pitting survivor against survivor in a zero-sum game. The really ugly involved the outcome of the arbitration: putting a price on people's pain.

The Good: Finding Voice and Affirmation

A significant minority of survivors looked favorably upon the arbitration process because they felt listened to and heard. These findings are consistent with Morgan (1999), May and Stengel (1990), and Bumiller (1988), who report that litigants want to use the legal process as a vehicle for voice. Although it was painful for survivors to discuss the details of the abuse, the arbitration itself seemed to be conducive to telling a thorough story. One advocate said that for some victims, "It was like flipping a switch. They would talk uninterrupted for two hours." The advocates unilaterally supported the idea that the arbitration could be a place to purge oneself of haunting memories, and all but one of the advocates talked about taking pains to construct a process that would empower victims. Specifically, many advocates encouraged survivors to bring family members, friends, or therapists, or to bring pictures of themselves as children, and they gave the survivors the option of having a Church representative present at the hearing. In this sense, most advocates recognized that the process of the arbitration was critically important. Survivors who felt positively about the arbitration generally used it to vent their innermost thoughts and feelings. George's comments illustrate this "voice for its own sake" mentality:

> ... I went in to that mediator, having to do the things I needed to do in the legal system—but I went into that mediation saying, "George, you better speak what you have to speak, emotionally, spiritually, psychologically, to finish, no matter what is going to happen outside, or with the settlement." I wasn't going in there to tell my story so that I could get some money. I was going in there so I could walk out of there knowing, "This is the end and whatever is unfinished might not have a chance to be finished." So I was going in there to finish, up to that point, my healing journey ... It was, "What do I need to do to heal?" And I did that. When I went in, I spoke from that place.

Greta, also unencumbered by any conflicting feelings about the utilitarian aspect of the arbitration, talked about the grace of having someone listen to her story without prejudice:

> [The arbitrator] didn't actually thank me, but he said something like, "I admire your honesty." He didn't say the words "thank you," but he did acknowledge me. He said, "Thank you for being so honest. I'm sorry this is so difficult. I will give the utmost consideration to everything you said. I paid close attention, I want you to know." He was sweet. I could feel him listening. I felt like he was on my side. I wanted to hug him.

Lydia, an advocate, talks about the power of the arbitration as a vehicle for voice, but notes at the outset that not all attorneys shared this perspective:

> Some attorneys (from what I heard) did just a question and answer: "Tell me this, tell me this, tell me this." Whereas most people [in this office], I believe, if not all, started out that way, but it became more of a conversation, the questions were more of, "Tell me a little bit about your background." "Were you a close family?" "What did you do for fun as kids?" To try to humanize the person in front of the arbitrator, to get them to understand their family and the role of religion in their lives. I remember [listening to the survivors] and I'm thinking about this wonderful little neighborhood, where the kids walked to and from church, where church was *fun*. And so they were really able to talk very poignantly about the pre-abuse period. And also very poignantly about the post-abuse and during-abuse period. *And that really helped the survivors to kind of complete the picture.* It helped the arbitrators. So I think that that process was very, very important. I remember times when I'm listening to the person talk and then they'd kind of finish their sentence and I'd have to kind of snap out of it because I was so intrigued! [laughs]

Several survivors felt that the arbitration had positively changed relationships in their lives. Douglas talked about how important it was that he could bring his sister to the arbitration to give her an opportunity to speak about her own experiences and how she was affected by the priest's actions. Similarly, Lewis explained that a family member disclosed during his arbitration that she also had been abused as a child, and that as a result of this communication, they understood each other much better. Both Connie[1] and Greta used this time to bring into the light the abuse they had been hiding for decades, explaining what had occurred graphically and in all of its ugliness. Like Lewis, they both claimed that the experience changed and strengthened their relationships with family members.

Several of the advocates talked about the arbitrators very positively as patient, kind individuals. Some commented that they had made affirming, empathic, supportive statements to the victims, such as "I believe you," "Thank you for sharing your story," or "You are incredibly strong."

> I remember this one judge who looked at this guy and said to one of the survivors, [slowly] "It's an honor to be in this room with you," and "You're a good man." (Lydia)

One advocate recalls his experiences in dozens of arbitrations:

> There was an interesting dynamic to this. These arbitrations started out
> where the arbitrators wouldn't say anything. These arbitrators were
> retired judges and had been through the system. They couldn't hold
> their tongues. Many of them were Catholic ... I can remember a
> number of them turning to the people and saying, "You're a hero to
> me." And it was a very powerful thing. (Trevor)

Because most of the survivors talked to me about the need for
validation, the arbitrators' comments were significant. Lynne, another
advocate, explains:

> They gave people credit that they deserved for coming forward, for
> being strong. And hearing that from your lawyer or hearing that from
> your therapist is one thing; hearing it from a stranger is another.

Lydia, an advocate, talks about the impact of the arbitrator's interaction:

> Things like that just ... were very powerful ... very simple words, but
> really were from the heart and really meant a tremendous amount to
> these men and women ... I think ... I mean, they meant a lot *to me*, so
> I think they meant a lot to the survivors. And my overall sense was
> that the survivors left feeling as though they were heard, they were
> understood, and their pain was understood and their experience was
> understood to the best of the arbitrator's ability from a participant's
> perspective.

These comments refine the previously discussed components of
procedural justice: they add the dimension of empathic impartiality. In
other words, it wasn't enough that people listened without prejudice, but
that the listener expressed, in some form—verbal or non-verbal—their
affirmation of the person telling the story. This empathy is particularly
important in cases where survivors feared that disclosure would create a
spoiled identity. Through empathic impartiality, some of the stigma of
the abuse was removed, some shame lifted.

The positive response, however, was not universal. Lynne, an
advocate, observes:

> It depended on what [the survivors] were expecting from the
> arbitration. If they had the feeling that, "I'll be able to tell this and life
> will change for the better," then that didn't happen for a lot of people.
> Other people have a better ability to compartmentalize. For them, they

came, they dumped their story, and they left and they felt really good, particularly when the arbitrator was able to validate them in some way.

In summary, then, for some survivors, using the arbitration as a forum to find one's voice had the potential to be a powerful, life-changing experience, as it had been for George, Greta, Virginia, and many other victims. But those who felt positively about the experience invariably had divorced the arbitration from the settlement, instead focusing on the catharsis of bearing truthful witness. When people mentally linked the process of arbitration to monetary compensation, their responses were decidedly less positive.

The Bad: Competition

In many of the clergy sexual abuse settlements, including the Boston Global Settlement and the Springfield settlement, a finite dollar amount was set and then divided up among the litigants. The steering committee was charged with disbursing the funds, and set up a matrix using various contextual abuse-related variables (e.g., the frequency and extent of abuse) and variables related to collateral damages (e.g., inability to work or maintain healthy relationships, history of alcoholism or substance abuse). Within set floor and ceiling amounts, a range of settlements was put into place. Based upon the notes from the arbitration and this matrix, each victim was assigned a dollar figure. While in theory this seems like a reasonable plan, in practice the plan translated into a zero-sum dynamic in which survivors were in competition with one another for a piece of the settlement pie. This generated tension marked a departure from the spirit of cooperation that linked the survivors, albeit sometimes loosely, throughout the litigation process. In the following passages, survivors talk about their feelings about the built-in competition:

> I had a hard time with the whole process. At some point I had made a decision that none of this was about money. But at this particular point, it was all about the money. Because of the way it was set up, there was a finite number being divided, so in my head, when I went in there, when it was my turn, every penny I got was one less my friend got. I had a huge problem. (Jeff)

> Like, I know a guy who was raped by [another priest] and he's in … treatment, you know. He's an alcoholic too, and he got, like, half as much. I mean, we don't talk about it; I never told another survivor how much I got, but he told me. And I figured out, he got like 100 and something [thousand]. And some people got far less. And that caused

me a little bit of—not guilt—but confusion, like, "Why [did I get more]?" But then I decided "I can't think about it." Maybe it was different arbitrators. I don't know. (Greta)

Although it wasn't intended to do so, it made it a contest. Who was worse? Who got hurt more? (Matthew)

Another survivor offers an alternative:

What I wanted to see, and I knew it wasn't going to happen, was the survivors to come together and say, "Let's just split it right down even and we'll all get it. And fuck this Church that is really playing with us." I understand that [the abuse] was different ... [stammers], that there are different [types], at some level. I don't know. (Anna)

After coming together to fight against injustice in the Church— arguably in a historic modern social movement—competition was distasteful for many victims, many of whom had come to know one another, and in many cases, even become friends.

The heart of these complaints involved a sense of both procedural and distributive injustice. Despite a general sense that the process was impartial, consistent, and ethical—which Tyler and Levanthal (1990) stress as critical— these survivors still felt that the last stage in the process and the outcome of that process, was not just. The crux of this injustice involved the separation of individuals from what many had come to see as their status as members of the survivor group. Herman (1997) speaks of this process of becoming interconnected with other survivors as integral to healing. To varying degrees, survivors had changed their "cognitive recognition" (Goffman 1963, p. 66). Leaving their isolation to become members of the same potentially "discreditable" group had lessened the stigma. Up to this last stage, the litigation helped alter their status as individual victims to survivors connected with others in pursuit of a common goal. By the end of the litigation, however, the final procedure positioned them against one another by making them compete for the settlement pie.

The Really Ugly: The Impact of Putting a Price on People's Pain

While many survivors were distressed by the dynamic that the settlement set up among victims, there were even bigger concerns about the dynamic the settlement created between victims and the Church. Although many felt that the arbitration process was positive—perhaps even cleansing—the product of the arbitration (i.e., the money) was much less appealing. The more damage a person could show, the more money he or she would be awarded. This translated into negative self-talk, which took a variety of forms.

The first form of negative self-talk involved the sense that they were pandering. Melissa talks about the effects of presenting herself as damaged:

> It's so weird. One of the problems that I had in my lawsuit was that, "You're a [member of a prestigious occupation[2]]. You're not suffering! Your life looks together to me! Why should you get any damages?" So I had to show that I was screwed up … Because you have to sell what you've been trying to overcome. Like, you have to maximize what you've been trying to overcome. … You get this strange kind of double consciousness of: "I'll show you, you can't ruin my life. I'll overcome this. I'll overcompensate and become a success." And on the other hand, you don't want to minimize the injuries done. Like, because they really *did* have an effect.

She adds:

> I think, and I've actually said in public … that I felt like a prostitute. Which I'm a little leery of having published; not because it isn't true, but because I don't want to make other victims feel bad. I don't want to add to the idea that victims are prostitutes because they take money in return for silence [due to earlier gag orders in settlements].

Fred talked about knowing that what he said eventually would translate into a dollar figure:

> When we go into [arbitration], that whole process is very painful. It's like prostituting yourself for the money. It makes me sick … I don't like it. It all comes down to what I do or say in the 20 minute scenario. [rhetorically:] That's how I'm going to be judged?

Howard speaks directly to this dynamic:

> And this wasn't about money! It was the shittiest thank you—the biggest Bo Jangles dance that I'll ever do in my life!

The more damaged a person could present himself or herself, the more money he or she received, a dynamic which flew in the faces of many victims' motivation to litigate to establish that they were not defective but, rather, caught in a traumatic situation. Roberta, a victim advocate, cogently sums up the paradox of trying to make the client look as defective as possible:

> I'd sit [in the arbitrations]. Again—it's an attorney kind of thing—I'd hear the attorney say to the arbitrator, "There's no hope of this person ever getting any better. They are going to live a damaged life." And you know where they are going with it, but the survivor is sitting there. And you're basically saying, [She motions to an imaginary person] "Your life is toast! You're done! ..." I guess they thought that was what they were supposed to do to get them more money. [rhetorically] Is that the best we can do? I don't think so. It just seemed inhumane.

This strategy—to portray the client to be as damaged as possible— seems diametrically opposed to survivors' needs. One survivor comments slightly more positively here on the complexity of this dynamic:

> But there was no chance to hear [in the arbitration hearing] how blessed you are, or "Yes, I'm an alcoholic but I'm sober and thank God." That doesn't matter. The point is, you're an alcoholic. Or that I tried to kill myself but that I'm alive now. That doesn't matter. And just hearing it, I tried to think of it as if this were someone else's life, being committed, and all the things that have happened, and being homeless. I was homeless. And just everything. For the first time ever I got it. This is my life. But not in a—how should I say this? Not in a way that made me feel bad about myself, but just to acknowledge the truth.

For some, the distinction between labeling the situation versus the individual as abnormal may have been lost. Insofar as it was, the arbitration process had the potential to be damaging for survivors.

Another form of negative self-talk involved minimizing one's own pain because other survivors received larger awards. Matthew provides a good illustration of this toxic inner process:

> [sarcastically:] Oh well, my injuries weren't so bad, so I didn't get that much. See, I'm less of a man ... Well, the range was 80 to 300k. I got 120k. That means I'm a big wuss because I complained about this. I'm a big sissy. The only way I would have felt any sense of redemption is if I had gotten the most. Then my pain would have been real. Now my pain is not.

Beleaguered by the often wearisome litigation process, many survivors were utterly deflated at the prospect of its conclusion being punctuated by a check. Lydia explains:

The people who were reluctant [to settle] were reluctant for reasons of, "I can't believe I did all of this. For two years I fought this hard and this is all that they are willing to give us!" You know, it was not a lot of money for what these people went through. And they weren't saying this out of greed. They were saying this out of, "Two years! I've lost my job, I've lost my wife, I've lost my kids, and all I'm going to get out of this is two-thirds of 300k!"

In summary, while victims across the board felt that they were owed something by the Church, they usually hated the idea that it boiled down to money.

What Survivors Really Wanted

Survivors almost uniformly agreed on a wide variety of things they wished had been accomplished through the settlement process: public acknowledgement of their pain, acceptance of responsibility for wrongdoing by the Church, an opportunity for voice (representativeness), and an apology. Unfortunately, these conditions are not typical in clergy sexual abuse litigation or other settlements. The agreement in the Boston settlement specifically states:

> It is further understood and agreed by Claimant that this Agreement is not to be construed as an admission of liability upon the part of any of the released parties [the Church and the offending priest] but rather as a good faith settlement of disputed claims.

It further specifies that the Church is released from liability from any of the mentioned matters "from the beginning of time."

While many survivors found this responsibility-evading language to be a jagged pill to swallow, it was less restrictive than the no-talk privacy clauses imposed in earlier settlements. Although it is not clear through this research, this language was almost certainly insisted upon by the Church. Historically, both no-talk clauses and the absence of responsibility-taking language are an effort on the part of defendants to limit their exposure to future litigation. While this language may be part and parcel of many settlements, it is not without its critics[3].

This legal maneuvering undercut the very motivations that propelled many survivors to litigate. One survivor explains the impact that such legalese has on victims:

> The other thing, too, is that—and I think that this is so important for litigation—is that the agreement, not to admit guilt, at the end of the

> [Boston] Global Settlement, this *legal fiction* that the crimes never occurred—is the worst thing for victims. It was sold by the lawyers as healing. So the end of the legal agreements—the settlements—contradict the very purpose of the lawsuit. (Elise)

The money, then, could not serve as a proxy for admission of guilt, an apology, or a variety of other survivors' hopes. Anna discusses the money almost as a consolation prize:

> And [victims] can't seem to get affirmation or acknowledgement or justice that this really even happened. And unfortunately, the civil system doesn't give it to them either, except that it does give them money. It does help.

Unfortunately, for most of the victims I spoke with, having the Church accept active responsibility fell off the radar screen in the course of the settlement negotiations, a practice very much in keeping with "the monetization of lawsuits" (Luban 1995, p. 2646). Here, two survivors discuss their desires to think outside the check:

> When I first met with the attorneys, it was like, "I don't want money. I just want [the Church] to pay my medical bills. I don't want anything beyond that. But I want them to donate money to SNAP. I want them to institute 'safe touch' programs in all of their parochial schools. I want them to look at their policies and put a victim on all of these boards." And I made those [things] part of my stipulations. And I can remember the lawyer going, "Where did you come up with this ridiculous stuff here?" Those things were so much more important to me than the others. And I ended up getting none of it. (Connie)

> You know, early on, I tried to persuade [my attorney] to include some non-monetary [options] and he didn't want to hear about it. He said, "That's not something ... maybe we can talk about that later." (Henry)

Most survivors had very distinct and creative ideas about what they would have liked to have happened in the course of settlement. Three clear themes emerged: restoration for the victim, incapacitation of offenders, and programming/activism for the community.

For The Victims

Acknowledgement
Many survivors felt a need to be acknowledged as human beings who had been terribly violated and harmed. Perhaps because the language of

the settlement agreement specified that the Church explicitly did not accept liability, the survivors I spoke with conveyed a longing for that type of acknowledgement. Moreover, the survivors desired that such acknowledgement be done publicly. Fred captures this emotion:

> [addressing the Church:] I am a survivor named Fred X that this happened to. And my mother is a devout Catholic. [The Church] needs to know that. You need to say something to me. You need to *feel* this problem. [rhetorically] How's that? You know what I mean? You need to say something to the people of the Church, not just victims. That you acknowledge this—not with a private check to a lawyer in settling the cases.

This theme also resonates in Rick's discussion about what he wished had happened in the settlement process:

> I wanted an apology from the priest, but the lawyer told me that if he ever did it, it would be an admission of guilt ... Survivors around here—or any survivors—want acknowledgement that something terrible and horrific has happened and they want the Church to accept the fact that something was done and, "What can [the Church] do to repair it?"

Melissa, not part of the Boston Global Settlement, did receive a letter from the Church acknowledging the harm it had allowed, and she articulates how important this was:

> [The Church] said, "We're sorry." But I'm more interested in the part [of the correspondence] that said, "... for the harm that was inflicted by Father X on you and your family." The next line, also, "For failing to comprehend the seriousness of your claim ..." So, they acknowledge 1) that the harm occurred, and 2) what happened was significant. So those are the two things that are being denied other victims.

Similarly, when asked what he would have liked to see in his settlement, Christopher responded:

> "I'm sorry," and an admission that they knew about these guys, because they did. And that it was just wrong and immoral to work with these people.

One survivor suggested a novel approach as a vehicle toward acknowledgement:

> We wanted printed in the publications [i.e., parish bulletins] once a
> month a Mass dedicated to survivors. And I had them put it in there.
> We did a lot of stuff that the lawyers [didn't think of]. (Vincent)

Another survivor suggested that, at the very highest levels, the Church
needed to acknowledge the harm that had been done:

> If I end up with a dead-end [in other advocacy work], I will take 5,000
> or so people and go right into St. Peters Square at the Vatican and
> make a spiritual statement. Not a violent one. Just call on them. *They
> can't deny you when you're in St. Peters Square.* We'll all wear the
> same color. Maybe on All Soul's Day. It could be international. It
> doesn't matter. They would have to acknowledge—one way or the
> other—that, "Hey, there's five thousand people out there wearing
> yellow. What's this about?" [To the Vatican:] "Are you gonna pray?
> Are you gonna come out and talk about this? It would be a statement
> one way or the other. Are you gonna stay in there? Come out and
> acknowledge it! Say something! Have a meeting. Do something! ...
> [now speaking to the Pope] You've got to see what's going on here,
> pal. Here's a group of people. Why don't you talk with them? See how
> they think and feel." Then they can't go home with a number. I'm a
> name. I'm a person. You saw me.

Buttressing this theme of acknowledgement were the anecdotes that
many advocates shared of survivors contacting them who did not wish to
pursue litigation:

> I mean, I had some clients who I didn't even put in a claim for! They
> said, "I don't want a claim, I don't want anything. But I knew Father X
> was a child molester because he molested me." These guys signed
> affidavits to support other people who wanted to make a claim. They
> just wanted to be counted and have their name [documented] ...
> (Gregory)

One survivor talked about the metaphysical burden of not knowing
how many victims had been silenced in earlier times who will never be
acknowledged:

> Oh, one thing other survivors have told me: We live [pause], and we
> have lived knowing there's more. There's more to the puzzle. It's a
> really intense thing to have to know. Some of the settlements, because
> they are settlements, *they are stuck in those papers*, they are stuck ...
> there is still stuff that hasn't been told. There is still stuff that *we know*
> inside our souls that hasn't been told. (George)

Voice

Some survivors hated to see the litigation come to an end because they felt it would quiet their newfound voices. They expressed a need to continue the dialogue that the litigation had created:

> I felt like I was going to lose my place at the table once I accepted money. I mean, I realized that I was going to lose my voice at the table anyway once the suits were settled anyway, that there wasn't going to be any table anymore! [laughs] But [pause, thinking] I really, really struggled with taking the money. I felt like, [slowly] I guess I don't totally understand the thinking. I felt that I wanted to be in an adversarial position with them. I didn't want to settle with them. I didn't want to say, "Yeah, you're off the hook." Because that wasn't what it was about for me. (Henry)

Another victim, who litigated prior to 2002, talks about his desire to be able to continue speaking about what had happened:

> I said [to my lawyer], "Look, I don't care about the money, I actually got what I was looking for, and that was to at least find out what was the truth and who knew what, when, about Father X. So I'll settle, but I would expect that I would at least be able to continue talking about what I learned." He said, "Well, a lot of cases have ["no talk" clauses]." (Aaron)

Somewhat surprisingly, only two survivors wished to confront their perpetrators. Here, Francis explains:

> But that's the one thing that I can't have and it would be neat if there was some way to allow me to confront him. If we weren't talking about 550 people in the lawsuit, I probably could have told [my attorney] to make that a condition of the lawsuit and make that happen, but that would have been unreasonable under the circumstances.

Apologies

Like a victim in the *A Civil Action* cancer cluster cases who said she began litigation because she wanted the head of Grace Corporation to "come to her door and apologize (Harr 1997, p. 452)," many victims wanted an apology from the Church. When asked what he would have liked to hear from the Church, Christopher replied: "'I'm sorry.' Really. It's that simple." Isaac echoes the importance of this:

> I've had a lot of unusual blessings, if you will. I know that sounds strange ... I received a formal apology from the bishop and received

an informal apology from one of the perpetrators, as well as a settlement. Really, in essence, I have received many blessings in that regard.

Although fairly accepted, the desire for an apology was not universal. Douglas explains his position:

I mean, [the money] is an empty gesture. It's like [the bishop] apologizing. There are some things that apologies are not accepted (sic).

Still, in this discussion, Douglas was the exception to the rule. Most survivors were looking for some sort of authentic apology and an acceptance of responsibility from the Church.

This research uncovered a unique postscript involving apologies in the Boston settlement. Interestingly, after the Boston Global Settlement had been completed, Archbishop Sean O'Malley wrote a letter to each of the litigants apologizing for the harm that had happened to each of them. However, because the Church was never privy to the litigants' personal information—address and phone number—, and because as part of the settlement they were barred from contacting the plaintiffs about this matter, the letters were sent in care of the corresponding attorneys in hopes that each would forward the letter to their clients. It is my understanding that some of the main firms did not forward the correspondence, leaving at least one-third of the "Global Settlement" clients without any idea that such a letter existed. I was able to ask one firm the reason for this, and they claimed that they did not want to intrude or interrupt their clients' lives with a reminder of the past. Tragically, this is precisely what many of the clients had wanted out of litigation. A similar conciliatory letter was written in another diocese, and it was reported that it was given out with settlement checks by one of the main firms involved. The advocates stated they felt the letter could be an important piece in their clients' healing journeys.

Programming/Additional Funding
Many dioceses, including Boston and Springfield, have policies that allow survivors to be reimbursed for therapy related to the abuse. However, many survivors and their advocates discussed the need for funding beyond therapy, or funding for more intensive therapy. For several survivors, the therapy reimbursements were limited to once a week for six months. One survivor had tried to procure scholarship funds for another survivor who had begun to put his life back together

and wanted to go back to college. He argued persuasively that the Church should pay for services that help survivors have a second chance at a normal life. Still, in other dioceses, it was difficult even to get therapy paid for.

The Boston Global Settlement includes a stipulation that the Office of Pastoral Support and Outreach will maintain therapy and specialized programming for survivors. However, because the Church was not allowed to reach out to the survivors individually, many survivors may not be aware of this programming.

For The Offenders: The Priest and The Church

Of the twenty-two victims with whom I spoke, the offending priest was dead in nine cases; in three cases, he was alive and incarcerated; in seven cases, he was alive and living in the community; and in five cases, the status of the offending priest was unknown[4].

Reactions from victims whose perpetrators were still at large and not under any justice agency supervision were somewhat mixed but, in general, tended not to be punitive. Only one victim, Matthew, would have liked to see his perpetrator imprisoned. The other six expressed a desire to keep the offender away from children first and foremost, but also, in many cases, to get some help for the offender. Perhaps the lack of vitriol toward the offending priests can be attributed to the age of the perpetrators—most were in their seventies or older; because of their age and frailty, they were viewed by the victims as more pathetic than anything else, although still a threat to society. In fact, most victims described their offenders as "sick" and not "evil." Commenting that her perpetrator was in his eighties, Elise's comments are typical:

> I want him to get treatment. And to be kept away from children. I want his superiors to be prosecuted. ... I still feel sorry for [this priest]. But I also know he's mentally ill. I believe the mentally ill need treatment. They don't need to be punished.

Henry tells a similar story:

> I wanted [the priest] to get help. I still felt something for him. But I wanted him to be out of a position where he could ever do this to someone else.

Several victims also talked about getting the perpetrators "off the payrolls" as a priority, as some priests were taken out of active ministry but were still supported financially by the Church. A few victims discussed the need to defrock priests (i.e., strip them of their status as priests) who had been found to have abused children, but neither of these was a major point for victims.

The sentiments expressed by victims whose perpetrators were dead or in prison were quite similar: Unilaterally, they believed the Church hierarchy's crimes dwarfed the crimes of the offending priests. Douglas captures the priorities of the majority of victims fairly explicitly:

> To me, the greatest atrocities were [the bishops] moving them around. [The priest] is just a sick fuck.

In all, survivors spent a great deal more time talking about the procedural crimes of the Church than about the offending priest. Clearly, interactions with Church officials, whether direct or indirect, stung. Freshly offended from hearing from so many others who had been similarly abused, victims were infuriated that the Church was aware of the abuse and had done little to prevent its recurrence.

The Community

The third set of goals involves the community: making information available, recognizing and working with secondary victims of abuse, and initiating legislative reforms regarding sex crimes. This section will deal with each of these topics, respectively.

As discussed in earlier chapters, establishing truth was a central goal for this litigation, and it was achieved most effectively through compulsory legal process, which released previously classified diocesan documents. Release of Church records has been made a part of settlements in some other jurisdictions. For example, the 2005 Orange County (CA) settlement specified that all of the documents would be released to the public in a schedule to be determined by the corresponding judge. Further, victims wanted transparency in record keeping going forward so that similar crises could not occur again.

A second recurring thread in survivors' narratives involved concern about the impact that the abuse had on other parties, including their immediate families and the Catholic and larger communities. Here, they reference what Ackerman (2002) talks about as restoring "harmony" between those affected and the larger community. Several survivors felt that disclosing the abuse had caused great anguish and conflict for their parents:

Here is another twist a lot of people don't understand: The old
Catholics in the old school, [my mother] goes back with canon law
before the Church to [Vatican II] 1962. There is something about "a
priest is never wrong." She's torn between her son being abused and
loving her son and not faulting the priest or she'll burn in hell ... She
literally believes that. Oh yeah. She won't tell me that, but that's what
goes on. A lot of these older Catholics can't tell you. They can't even
tell you what they're going through. And they're all disgusted. Their
whole faith system has been cracked. And I'm mad—not only for the
children—but now I'm mad at this part of it. Because of the
hierarchy's distance, quietness—whatever you want to call it—it's
outraging these good Catholic praying people. And they don't know
what to do. They sit privately in their homes and they are disgusted,
angry and hurt. (Fred)

Lawrence, Louis, Edward, Greta, Anna, Virginia, Beth, Howard,
Andrew, Douglas, Fred, Rick, Connie, and Christopher talked
poignantly about the strain that the abuse revelations had put on their
family members. Several talked about the need for these family
members to be covered for costs of therapy relating to the abuse as well.
In fact, in one of the settlements, therapy for family members was
included. Howard discusses the impact on the larger community:

There is a woman, a proverbial, quintessential woman who sits in the
right hand side of the church every Sunday—if I ever go in the
church—and she's never done a fucking thing wrong. She's given her
money, she's believed, she's developed a wisdom in her faith.
[Disgusted tone:] What do you think this [scandal] has done to *her*?

Howard's comment touches upon the impact felt by the larger Catholic
community, shaken by a scandal previously unfathomable. Their faith,
worldviews, and sensibilities have been rocked by the revelations that
the Catholic Church acted in such a reckless manner toward the most
vulnerable members of its community. Several people mentioned the
number of secondary victims who needed healing because of the
scandal, and indicated that the Church should have an obligation to
respond to them as well.

Legislative Action
In addition to addressing family and community needs, survivors and
their advocates spoke passionately about making substantive legislative
changes that would ensure victims' rights. The 2002 scandal sparked a
frenzy of legislative activity both in Massachusetts and elsewhere, most
of which dealt with elimination or amendment of the statute of

limitations for rape and other crimes involving sexual abuse. Herman describes how survivors may find a "mission" as one of the final stages of healing. By "transcending" the trauma, they make it "a gift" to others in the form of prevention or awareness work (1997, p. 179).

At the time of the Boston litigation, the law in Massachusetts placed a six-year cap on criminal actions and a three-year cap from the age of majority (18) on civil actions for childhood-sexual-abuse-related crimes, with a discovery rule exception on the civil side that states that the clock begins to run when a reasonable person "discovered or should have discovered that an emotional or psychological injury or condition was caused by said act" (General Laws C. 260, statute 4c). In a move that significantly constricted the discovery rule, *Doe v. Creighton* (2003) specified that any person attempting to use the discovery rule bears the burden of affirmatively proving that an objective person would have failed to see the causal connection. The court writes:

> This is not, however, a subjective test; the only individualized characteristics that we consider in making a reasonable person analysis under G.L. C. 20 statute 4c, are those that stem directly from the complained-of tort. Personal traits unrelated to the tort, such as cultural background and educational history, are not relevant to the reasonableness inquiry. We focus on the nature of the abusive conduct, the injuries that the abuse inflicted, and the effect that both would have had on the causal understanding of an ordinary, reasonable person (439 Mass. 281).

Further, the court noted that Doe's abuse began at an older age, sixteen, and found that the plaintiff should have been more aware than a much younger child, signaling an important benchmark for the reasonableness standard.

Perhaps because the litigation spawned by the 2002 Catholic Church scandal was filed before this ruling, the ruling did not seem to bear heavily upon the Global Settlement. Because of the politics of the consolidated litigation, there were several cases that were well beyond the statute of limitations discovery rule, but that were included nonetheless in the settlement. However, the constrictions for filing in civil court, whether involving the actual statute of limitations or the discovery rule, became a flashpoint for activism for many survivors. With the expert testimony of several survivors, no less than five separate bills were submitted to the Massachusetts Legislature for review in 2004 (Massachusetts House Bills 1892-1896, 2004).

In general, the respondents I spoke with—both advocates and attorneys— supported some change to the criminal and civil statutes of limitations. Twice as many respondents (18) desired both statutes to be eliminated, while a significant minority (9) suggested either an extended or more nuanced statute would be appropriate. In cases where respondents wanted the statute repealed, the arguments often centered around analogizing such crimes to murder, which currently has no such limitations:

> I don't think that there should be [a statute of limitations for criminal or civil suits]. I equate this with murder ... It metaphorically or symbolically killed whoever I was going to be, you know, forever. Would I have been an alcoholic? What kind of dad would I have been? All—some of those choices were—I'm not going to say taken away because I don't want to shift all of the blame to them either—were limited. It kind of limited what I could do. (Christopher)

> To me, it's equivalent to murder ... And I don't see any difference between committing murder [and child sexual abuse], in which case, there is—despite the fact that a defendant will be prejudiced by loss of evidence and all that—they still can be tried, years later if they are still alive. But I really don't see any difference between that and sexual assault of a minor. To me, its little legal considerations of how would someone get the best evidence just don't compare in any way to the moral issue of what was done to someone. (Justine)

> My answer would be no, there should be no statute of limitations for something like this, but that may be because I was directly affected. I just think that certain types of things, there should be no statute of limitations. Murder. There's no statute of limitations. Sexual crimes, there should not be a statute of limitations. Maybe if you rob a store and fifteen years go by, ok, you got away with it. But, violent crimes, I don't think there should be a statute. (Matthew)

> When a child is assaulted, it's a charge against humanity as a whole because that is the future. That's our future. When you assault a little boy or a little girl, you put something where it doesn't belong, that's a charge against humanity. [almost spitting] Like Hitler did and the rest of those knuckleheads. (Rick)

Citing the long-term effects of the trauma, one advocate states:

> While the crime may have been committed twenty or thirty years ago, the pain and consequences are still present. (Marvin)

Another advocate goes even further, stating that if only one crime did not have a statute of limitations, it should be child sexual abuse, not murder. He opined that with such cases, the traumatic effects are life-long and tremendously consequential.

Several survivors and their advocates discussed the factors that conspire to ensure the victim's silence as another reason to eliminate the statute:

> Sexual abuse is the perfect crime because while the perpetrator is committing the crime, he is also taking away the ability of that person to tell anyone about what happened. That is why revisions to the civil and criminal statute of limitations are needed. (Walter)

> I was 38 when my memories came. I think late thirties or early forties is a very typical time for memories to come back. (Anna)

> I mean, you forgot [the abuse] for a reason: because your psyche couldn't handle it. It waits till a point where you could handle it to let it burst through. But even then it's three years past when you remember. But that's a drop in the bucket towards being strong enough. (Beth)

> From my own experience I know that, um, it took me twenty years to even identify, even though I didn't forget about it. I knew about it. I knew what it was. I had no clue that it had the impact it had on me. (Henry)

Lewis, noting that the statute robs people of the acknowledgement of what happened, puts it succinctly: "It's like a pencil eraser. How can we live like that?"

Justine discusses the unreasonableness of the new standard set forth in *Doe v. Creighton*:

> And the whole thing about the subjective test—it is, "What would an objectively reasonable person do who was in this condition, who was sexually abused?" And the minute you get that person, they are no longer the objective reasonable person. And who has not had that experience can say, "Well, but I would have … Having been *raped* as a child on the altar, I would still be able at age 23 to say, 'Yes, I was ready.'" I don't think anyone can be there, in the other person's position.

She talks about due process concerns, and why eliminating the statute would not infringe on them:

> The reasons for the statute of limitations are to give the defendants a chance to not suffer a loss of evidence. In these kinds of cases, where

it's almost always going to be just one person's testimony, that's not really such a concern. To me, that is such a subordinate concern, and I think that if someone is saying, "This happened to me 30 years ago," I think people have a natural inclination to really question that kind of testimony anyway. So, in some ways, I think the safeguard is already there, just through the natural process. (Justine)

Not all survivors, however, wanted the statute of limitations abolished. A few argued that it should be extended, but not eliminated, citing the need for due process and its importance in a democracy:

I've been asked to get involved with [repealing the statute] and I won't. I really don't support that. I mean, I'm not saying I'm totally opposed to any adjustment … but we have a statute of limitations for a reason. And maybe the numbers attached to it might be arbitrary, but the fact that we have one isn't some arbitrary decision on somebody's part. Having no statute of limitations I think would be dangerous, terrible. I [work with children]. If someone came in 25 years [from now] with some false charge against me, how am I supposed to defend myself? In our culture everyone assumes that it is true. I'm just thinking that there's a reason why we have it. (Francis)

Finally, a small minority of survivors (3) talked about the statute of limitations as simply barking up the wrong tree in terms of advocacy work for victims. Howard, after ceding that the laws need to be amended to allow more time, talks more philosophically about the legislative battle overall:

How can you argue with it? It [would be] a good law to pass. And so I think that the problem is … It benefits a lawyer. How does it benefit a client? It doesn't, really. Because, what it still does is keep them in a flawed system, it allows people to use these types of civil lawsuits to fight the wrong battles. There is not a justice system that goes with it.

After noting the importance of eliminating the limitations on the criminal statute, Marilyn echoes Howard's comments about "fighting the wrong battles:"

As far as the civil litigation goes, I just don't really believe in the retributive model of justice anymore. I hope as a country, and a world, that we are realizing more of a restorative community approach to offenses.

Interestingly, only two people made any distinction between civil and criminal statutes. With these exceptions, anyone who wanted the criminal statute repealed also wanted the civil one abolished.

Other legislative efforts survivors were involved in centered around amending the charitable immunity cap, which at the time of the Boston Global Settlement was only $20 thousand in Massachusetts. When survivors became aware of this cap, they felt strongly that the amount be raised. Or, alternately, some suggested that an exception could be created when the subject of the tort is criminal activity. In other words, if someone slips and falls outside a hospital, the liability cap would remain intact; however, if doctors are molesting patients with supervising personnel aware of their actions, the cap would be forfeited.

---

[1] In Connie's case, she told her full story at a court hearing, not arbitration.

[2] Her occupation has been deleted to protect her identity.

[3] Specifically, legal scholars Richard Zitrin (1999), David Luban (1995), and Carrie Menkel-Meadow (1995) argue that court-sponsored secrecy in particular may shield the public from information that may be necessary for public health. For instance, the early asbestos, Bridgestone/Firestone, and Dalkon Shield cases all involved secrecy clauses that—had the information not remained sealed—could have saved other lives (Givelber and Robbins 2006). It is unlikely that people would have continued using such devices if they were aware of the potential hazards involved. The same arguments have been applied to the clergy sexual abuse cases that stipulate the victims must remain silent about the litigation (Fiftal 2003): if others had known that a particular priest had been the subject of sexual abuse lawsuits—or that the Church had admitted to such behavior—it is doubtful that they would have allowed their children access to such men.

[4] The number is greater than twenty-two because in two cases, there was more than one perpetrator.

9
Conclusions

Have I reached justice? There is no justice. There is no justice. Have I reached satisfaction? I would say that I've reached a level of satisfaction. But justice? There is nothing fair or equitable. Justice? Give me back my ... [trails off]. You know what? Change the memories of what I've seen, what I've felt, what I've done the last thirty years. That's justice. There is no justice. There's a satisfaction of changing an institution, changing society. But justice? My God, I hope not. If this is justice, God help us. (Jeffrey)

There are many lessons to be learned from the clergy sexual abuse survivors and advocates with whom I spoke. First and foremost, there is a gravity to this litigation that transcends the average personal injury tort. Because of the nexus of damaging features of this type of abuse—its mixture with religion, notions of sinfulness and (sometimes) homosexuality, the wild asymmetry in power—clergy sexual abuse can only be described, albeit inadequately, as devastating. Survivors spoke to me about the resultant trajectories of their lives with an intensity I could not have anticipated; advocates presented themselves as traumatized witnesses to unimaginable atrocities. Even I, hearing the stories of corrosive shame and dashed hopes, often wept over the loss of innocence that survivors and their families were left with which to deal. With that understanding, it is important to realize that litigation was life-defining for many survivors. For many, it facilitated a transformation in their identities: from rebellious to heroic, vulnerable to strong, solitary to partnered, or shameful to proud. Other survivors, however, did not fare as well.

The survivors I spoke with were a diverse group. They were educated, uneducated, accomplished, underachieving, stable, nomadic, poor, wealthy, from loving homes, and from highly dysfunctional homes. The common thread among them was an alienation from the Church. The realization that their Church had forsaken their trust and their innocence was crushing to them, and when the social distance between survivors and the Church grew, the seeds of rebellion and defiance took root. Through the coupling of defiant pride with a crisis of legitimacy in the Church, victims transformed themselves into survivors through the act of initiating litigation. David (or many Davids, acting in concert) had a chance to triumph over Goliath.

As posited in defiance theory (Sherman 1993), these four ingredients—social distance, illegitimacy, shame, and pride—help to explain why so many victims went forward to litigate against the Church, an ultimate act of defiance against what they believed to be an illegitimate agent. These considerations largely put to rest the utility of a rational calculus model in understanding these litigation goals. Perhaps more importantly, they illustrate the importance of emotion and relationships in shaping the transformation of disputes.

Early Meaning

At the outset, the litigation promised these survivors an opportunity to put their shame and negative emotions to use. For many, it provided a key to maps of their lives that helped them reorganize and make sense of their emotions and experiences, changing the indications they made to themselves about their own nature (Blumer 1969). Litigation became a vehicle for them to transform their identities. It caused them to reconsider blame and responsibility; instead of feeling like screw ups or failures, they came to understand that their lives had been shaped in irrevocable ways by forces beyond their control. It gave them the opportunity to find their "brothers" or "sisters" with similar pasts, the opportunity to feel normal, and the opportunity to shed some of the stigma (Goffman 1963) they had carried throughout their lives. For some survivors, being with their peers marked the first time they felt comfortable in their own skins. These new relationships proved particularly important in the transformation of disputes; because of them, the litigation took on a new, forward-looking meaning for many survivors.

Perhaps one of the most robust findings of this research is that so many survivors entered into litigation with the ambition of establishing truth. Some wanted to establish truth for themselves, exorcising demons of insecurity and shame; others wanted to establish truth for their newly found brethren, to support each other. Still others wanted to establish truth for the benefit and protection of others. Many survivors wanted to be able to bear truthful witness to history. As I have come to understand, truth is what these survivors looked for when they had nothing else; it was the bedrock upon which prevention, fraternity, and peace could be built.

These survivors helped me understand that this litigation is more about voice than a monetary settlement. In this sense, Tyler's theory (1990), which set forth the components of procedural justice, is relevant, particularly with respect to the need for representativeness. Survivors yearned to be able to have a voice, and to be dealt with honestly and ethically, without stigma or shame. Because of this, it is imperative that attorneys and the Church understand that implementing secrecy clauses which serve to make the victim feel he or she has done something wrong or has taken part in something shameful can re-traumatize survivors. Such actions represent a final insult in the formal transformation of disputes continuum: diminishing any potential personal strength the survivor may have gained and casting a long pall on the process.

Complex Relationships

Many advocates I spoke with understood that survivors approach litigation as a tool of voice and empowerment. In cases of childhood sexual trauma in particular, victims often feel as if the experience and its consequences are totally outside of their locus of control. Unfortunately, the nature of collective representation often confounds these feelings, as attorneys often did not maintain regular contact with their clients. Many survivors had to rely on the media to learn of new discoveries or developments in their cases, leaving them feeling powerless once again over major events in their lives. Still, the good news was that, in Boston at least, many speculated that the goal of establishing truth was achieved—to greater or lesser extent.

The advocates who worked for these victims provided an outstanding service in the simple act of listening to their stories. Attorneys were often the first to bear witness for these survivors. Because they met people often at their most vulnerable, they played a critical role in the survivor's life and perspectives on healing. In particular, their sensitivity was consequential. It is my understanding, through this study, that there were attorneys who displayed great empathy and knowledge about sexual abuse. Those who worked closely with social workers or had them as part of their staff, in particular, seemed most in tune with the needs of this population.

Closure

The remaining course of litigation, including settlement, was often disappointing for survivors. Having achieved some social recognition that they were not alone in their experiences, survivors were left to contemplate the meaning of litigation in a game where money was typically the outcome over which the attorneys on both sides had battled. Survivors' concerns were with both procedural (process) and distributive (end goal) justice. That closure came with a check—however much it might be—was deflating to many survivors. Further, survivors loathed the feeling of competition that the disbursement process engendered. When survivors were able to divorce the arbitration process from the end result (i.e., a check), they appreciated the opportunity for voice and validation that it provided, and there were several powerful accounts of survivors finding that process both positive and transformative. Still, the conclusion loomed large, and a check for some victims was, at best, useful; at worst, dirty. Most survivors abandoned the notion that civil litigation could bring about fairness or justice. Some—usually those connected to their peers—redirected their energies into advocacy work; others became disillusioned and bitter. In the end, both David and Goliath would be left battered and bruised, but there would be no clear winner.

Survivors eloquently described to me what it was they had hoped for at the conclusion of their litigation, and perhaps there is no better way to convey this but to let them speak for themselves. In contrast to goals of retribution or revenge, the three most common themes they spoke about were more in line with restorative goals (Braithwaite 1998): prevention, acknowledgement, and apologies. The following comments capture what many, if not most, survivors were looking for.

On prevention:

> When I first met with the attorneys, it was like, "I don't want money. I just want them to pay my medical bills. I don't want anything beyond that. But I want them to donate money to SNAP. I want them to institute 'safe touch' programs in all of their parochial schools. I want them to look at their policies and put a victim on all of these boards." (Connie)

On acknowledgement:

> Survivors around here—or any survivors—want acknowledgement that something terrible and horrific has happened and they want the

Church to accept the fact that something was done and, "What can [the Church] do to repair it?" (Rick)

On apologies:

I don't mean to oversimplify, but if someone had looked at us face-to-face and said, "I'm so terribly sorry," it could have changed things. (Norman)

Because of these and other similar sentiments, it would seem fitting that future litigation attempt to think outside the check when considering settlement. It is feasible that attorneys use the tort process to fashion atypical settlements to achieve a more satisfying outcome for their clients. This may involve some restorative justice processes; it may not. In either case, survivors should be deeply involved in the details and stipulations of the settlement. In many cases, non-pecuniary objectives are most meaningful to litigants. Attorneys should be prepared to talk about these possibilities during settlement.

Looking Forward

Perhaps some of the best practices can be gleaned both from the experiences of the people I spoke with, as well as from the case of three orphanages in Canada that had more than 700 allegations of abuse lodged against them over a thirty year span. Like Boston and most other dioceses beset by scandal, there was a paper trail of allegations and quiet investigations that circumvented criminal proceedings. In the early 1990s, 400 of the students formed a mutual support group, HELPLINE, to explore alternative resolutions. Through mediation in 1992, an agreement was reached with the Brothers of the Christian Schools in Ottawa, the government of Ontario, and the Archdiocese that included apologies from those responsible, financial compensation involving $23 million (Canadian) dollars, financial advances for medical and dental needs, money for vocational, educational, and literacy training, back pay for work completed during the children's occupancy, and a commitment to work to abolish child abuse. These terms seem more in line with the types of goals that survivors expressed to me. While money was still involved in that settlement, it was situated within a larger, forward-facing settlement package that attempted to assist survivors to succeed in specific areas of their lives (Gavrielides and Coker 2005; Robinson 2002). Indeed, there is much from this history that can be brought to bear on future clergy sexual abuse cases.

In addition to some of the forward-looking alternatives from Canada, there are things law firms can do to improve services for survivors. Simply put, attorneys who manage these cases must have a formalized protocol for handling the therapeutic needs of their clients. Law school cannot prepare advocates for the types of issues that invariably will present themselves in these types of cases. Ad hoc referrals are not sufficient; by definition, these cases involve significant abuse. Firms need to either have a social worker on staff, or maintain formalized relationships with service providers so that clients can expedite attending to human service needs, including problems with shelter and healthcare, as well as therapy. Firms involved in this work should also consider peer referrals as part of their mission for those clients who are eligible (i.e., whose legal needs do not conflict) and willing. The connections that survivors forged with each other, with or without the help of attorneys were transformative and life-affirming for many survivors with whom I spoke.

Further, attorneys should reconsider the language of settlements, which includes stipulations that the conclusions are not an admission of fault. This is, without question, one of the most tragic pieces of the resolutions of these cases. In this sense, the clergy sexual abuse litigants I spoke with seemed to have a good deal in common with other litigants who fared considerably differently in terms of settlement. Despite sharp financial differences between settlements in *A Civil Action*—who received more than the average Boston clergy abuse litigants, totaling over $450,000—and *Agent Orange* litigants—who averaged significantly less, with some as little as a few hundred dollars—(Harr 1995; Schuck 1987), the overarching theme among these litigants seems to be a disillusionment with the idea that civil litigation can achieve justice. Perhaps some of this disappointment lies with the idea that the absence of active responsibility philosophically leaves the dispute to remain in the "blaming" stage indefinitely. Survivors need to hear someone accept ownership for the wrongs committed. This may mean hearing a Church representative admit fault, or it may mean including language in the settlement to that effect. It would be advantageous for attorneys in future cases to look into an option of including responsibility-taking language, while at the same time allowing releases for the Church from future litigation.

Survivors also discussed the statutes of limitation as a focal point for advocacy. Nearly every survivor, and all of the advocates, agreed that changes needed to be made to the statute. Some adamantly argued that the statute should be eliminated for sex crimes involving a child, while others suggested that both the civil and criminal statutes could be extended in appreciation of the difficultly that victims face when considering whether to disclose the abuse. Given what we have come to understand about the nature of childhood sexual abuse and its psychological consequences, an extension of the statute regarding childhood sexual abuse seems the least that could be done to improve the rights of survivors.[1]

Litigation is often thought of as the end point in the transformation of disputes (Felstiner et al. 1980-1981). This study makes clear that litigation may be the beginning of a complex stage, with its own shifts in emotions and goals—a launching pad for soul-searching transformation. While the formal legal process may have come to a close, the personal and social transformation that occurred for many has only begun. While most entered litigation trying to establish truth, many moved on to work for justice that had little to do with settlement. More broadly, litigation can be framed as a transformation continuum in its own right, not merely the conclusion in a transformation of disputes.

The maxim about "what doesn't kill you makes you stronger" bears consideration here. The literature on trauma compellingly states how finding a victim mission is a key to healing for many victims (Herman 1997). Litigation that involves some type of life trauma or significant loss can become an opportunity for personal and social transformation. Just as drug addicts can make powerful drug counselors, or war veterans compelling war protestors, these survivors found the key to transforming themselves in accepting, overcoming, and using the trauma they experienced for others' benefit. The litigation process can foster such transformation through restorative processes that empower victims, or impede it through the use of traditional responsibility-evading language or poor attorney/client communication. Litigation needs to be a process whereby survivors are able to reclaim some control. At a bare minimum, however, it should be able to forge some truth simply by bringing the appropriate parties to the table.

Not every survivor I spoke with became an activist; sadly, those who felt little connection to their peers were sometimes left behind, alone with new trauma in their lives stirred up through the litigation. Their disillusionment, without support from others, has the potential to turn into despair. I suspect the survivors I spoke with may have been further along in their healing processes than other survivors because they were able to talk to me, an outsider. Still, even those survivors who I spoke with who had not formally connected to their peers felt some pride in knowing their litigation may provide solace for other victims, many of whom may never come forward to disclose, let alone litigate.

This study has only begun to look at the phenomenon of clergy sexual abuse litigation. It does not, nor did it ever intend to, adequately study the phenomenon of the abuse itself, the impact of which is difficult to comprehend. Without question, this is a group of survivors that merits more study so that services can be improved to meet their needs.

In closing, I must add that it is with deep sadness that I report that some members of the Church hierarchy continue to fight the truth of these stories. The Vatican's response in early 2010, calling it petty gossip (Tran 2010) and comparing the Church's pain from unfavorable media exposure to the persecution of the Jews (Owen and Boyes 2010), will only cause the survivors more pain, and ironically, probably propel more people to litigate against the Church.

At the time of this writing, countless dioceses across the country and in Europe are currently embroiled in litigation centered around clergy sexual abuse. The end is nowhere in sight. Although media coverage of these cases waxes and wanes, their frequency has not. Given this, it may be prudent to reflect on the ambitions of the survivors in initiating litigation to establish truth. Legal scholar Martha Minow writes:

> Some say: Individuals, and nations, can have too much memory. Perhaps this only happens when it is the wrong kind of memory: superficial, or overflowing without a catch basin. Or perhaps it happens when the truth attends to a past without affording a bridge to the future (2004, p. 62).

It is important that both attorneys and the Church recognize that litigation did afford an opportunity for memory, but all involved must insure that this community memory does not simply "overflow without a catch basin." The memory uncovered since 2002 is a powerful history, but not the end of the story. One of the common misconceptions that survivors wanted other people to understand was that their pain was not over because they had settled. The settlement might have been the first step in a very long healing process (Cullen 2004). As such, the memory must be honored and preserved, so that a lasting legacy is begun, and a bridge to the future is built.

---

[1] This could be done in several ways. One way to lessen restrictions would be to raise the age for the statute well into adulthood, as opposed to twenty-one in Massachusetts. For instance, in Connecticut, adults who have been abused as children have until their forty-eighth birthday to file suit (Newman 2006). Alternately, changing the objective test also would remove some of the barriers

to filing suit. Also, extending the discovery rule to six or more years also would allow for more leeway for potential litigants.

Appendix A
Methodology

Very simply put, the only way to get [empirical validation] is to go directly to the empirical, social world—to see through meticulous examination of it whether one's premises or root images of it, one's questions and problems posed for it, the data one chooses out of it, the concepts through which one sees and analyzes it, and the interpretations one applies to it are actually borne out. (Blumer 1963, p. 32).

Blumer wrote that symbolic interactionism strives to, "respect the nature of the empirical world and organize a methodological stance to reflect that respect" (1963, p. 60). This study examines the meaning of clergy sexual abuse litigation by going directly to the empirical world—from the position of the direct actors involved in it. I have conducted face-to-face interviews with men and women who have litigated against the Catholic Church, as well as their advocates, due to allegations of sexual abuse by priests. The methodology, consistent with feminist inquiry, should facilitate the development of knowledge, and allow for subsequent theory building in an area where little prior research exists.

During 2004 and 2005, I conducted face-to-face interviews with twenty-two men and women who litigated against the Catholic Church, as well as thirteen plaintiffs' attorneys and other legal advocates. These interviews occurred through a combination of sampling from attorney-client lists, as well as through a snowball sampling technique. Initially, I made contact with plaintiffs' attorneys, and, with their endorsement, they sent letters outlining the study and inviting their clients' participation. Only a few survivors came forward through this method. I then met with members of the lay Catholic group Voice of the Faithful, who agreed to spread the word about my research. From these contacts, several key survivors reached out to me. These survivors were supportive of efforts to study and understand the issues involved in clergy sexual abuse disclosure and litigation, and subsequently sent emails to fellow survivors telling them about the research and expressing their views that I was particularly sensitive to victim issues. After trust was established with these initial interviewees, subsequent interviewees came forth in greater numbers and the research gained momentum. In hindsight, it is not surprising that word-of-mouth within the survivor community was more productive than the mailing strategy, given the survivors' experiences with intimate betrayal (see also Weihe and Richards 1995 for a discussion on intimate betrayal).

Early in the interview[1], I often allowed respondents to follow their own journey, asking only follow-up or paraphrasing questions for clarity, a strategy set out by Reissman (1993). This strategy accomplished several things: first, it allowed the participant to speak, generally uninterrupted, with a skilled listener. Next, it relaxed the participant by showing that the interview would not adhere to a strict format. Simply put, because the theoretical framework of this study involves understanding the meaning of events, it was important that respondents be allowed to complete their own thoughts. I very much saw my job as one of following them, wherever their logic might lead. Often, I found this interview style often covered much of the protocol without a great deal of prompting. Usually in the second half of the interview I made sure that the topics were covered comprehensively, following up where things had been vague. As Weiss (1994, p. 42) points out, this "diachronic" format allows the respondent to build a chronology of the post-victimization experience. In contrast to more structured interviews where researchers may try to keep to a "point," the interview process used here is conducive to "story telling" as a form of uncovering meaning (Mischler 1986, p. 69).

Notably, I did not ask about the actual sexual abuse experience. The interviews focused on survivors' subjective experiences of self and the meanings and interpretations they attached to the abuser, the church, the justice system, the survivor community, and other individuals and groups over the often protracted period from initial disclosure to final settlement.

Interviews with legal advocates focused on their understandings of plaintiff motivations, the nature of mass tort litigation, lawsuit proceedings and settlements, and interactions with survivor-clients. These interviews were conducted with attorneys, social workers, and paralegals from multiple law firms, as well as local and national advocates from the survivor community. Because both survivors and their advocates were interviewed, I was able to triangulate much of the information that was relayed regarding the initiation, course, and settlement of these cases.

Interestingly, I was able to triangulate the data on several occasions, sometimes intentionally, sometimes not. Specifically, there were several instances where I independently interviewed people who had witnessed similar events or disclosures[2]. Because many of the people I interviewed knew one another, but often did not know that I knew the other person, I heard several of the same stories from multiple respondents, providing a point of corroboration. A second source of triangulation involved using media articles—and in a few cases, online testimonials on an advocacy website—to corroborate stories. Although not every account reported to me was verified by another source, the fact that many were was reassuring.

On average, the interviews lasted about two hours, although there were some that extended to three or four hours. Both the advocates and the survivors were generally eager to talk, in many cases to unload what had been an incredible journey. Each interview with survivors began with a few questions about the respondent's family background and early involvement with the Catholic Church, starting with a broad statement like, "Tell me about what role the Church played in your and your family's lives growing up." The next stage of the interview focused on how and to whom the respondent initially disclosed his or her victimization(s) (if at all), the person's reactions, and the respondent's responses to those reactions.

In several instances, disclosure took place in several contexts prior to the initiation of the litigation, and each of these disclosures, and their meaning to respondents, was explored. The final stage of the interview focused on the litigation process, the respondent's quest for justice—however he or she defined it—and the respondent's reflections on the course and settlement of the litigation. The amount of time given to each topic was determined by the particular details of each individual's story, and the personal salience of particular issues. The interviews were characterized by a relaxed, conversational style and produced a case history for each respondent (Weiss 1994).

The interviews were tape-recorded, transcribed verbatim, and the transcripts were subsequently checked for accuracy and completeness. The transcripts were then organized and coded using Q6 qualitative software, and analyzed to identify and articulate important themes, events, perceptions, and understandings.

Finally, it is important to note the lengths I went to protect the identity of the subjects involved in this research. Immediately after the interview, I assigned an initial pseudonym to use in transcription so that the person's true identity was never on any of the field-notes. Next, at the conclusion of all of the transcriptions, a research broker (Lee 1993) drew up a list of names to be designated as second pseudonyms. The lists connecting the pseudonyms were then destroyed, so that I would have no way to conclusively link the final field-notes to any particular interview[3]. All tapes from interviews have since been destroyed as an additional measure of protection.

Validity

Within any empirical research, validity is a high-ordered concern. Although I extensively discuss these considerations in my dissertation, in the interests of time and space, I will discuss in this section only what I believe to be some of the most essential pieces.

First, the crux of internal validity in an exploratory, qualitative study like this lies in the rapport between researcher and survivor, specifically in the candor that the relationship can foster from the participants. As Felstiner et al. (1980-1981) note,

> Since the study of transformations must focus on the minds of the respondents, their attitudes, feelings, objectives, and motives ... [it must be] based upon a high level of rapport between the researcher and the informant (pp. 652-653).

Fortunately, the response to being part of the study was overwhelmingly positive. Although it is impossible to determine the extent to which subjects withheld information—particularly given the sensitivity of many topics—my impressions are that they were remarkably candid about their experiences and the meanings they held for them. In general, there was a high level of rapport. I have experience working with survivors in direct services, and I saw my job as one to listen patiently and intently. Reisman (1993, p. 4) notes that "the research interviewer can also bear witness," and I found this to be true in this project. The interviews were often emotional and intense for both researcher and participant, and many survivors expressed gratitude for the opportunity to tell their stories.

As in any study, respondents may exaggerate or lie to present a socially desirable impression. Participants in this research all had some role in high-stakes litigation. All of them—save a few of the advocates—obtained, at minimum, $17,000 through the settlement; more typically between $50,000 and $200,000 after lawyers' fees. The perception that these survivors, and some attorneys, were opportunistic was real, and most spoke to this stereotype and tried to dispel it. In general, I tried to get beyond some of these issues by nonjudgmental probing. My hope was that this approach allowed people to relax enough to be honest in their responses. Perhaps the best example of this was when people would tell me the litigation wasn't about the money, and most people were quick to report this. With gentle probing, this initial response usually gave way to a confluence of mixed emotions about the litigation. Most people were able to articulate a multiplicity of motives and meanings. Further, most were able to acknowledge that at some point during settlement negotiations, it *was* all about the money. That most people were able to acknowledge this to me—something that perhaps might be construed negatively—was a testament to the rapport established in the interview. Although this did not happen in every case, it happened quite often. This level of rapport hopefully speaks to the validity of the study.

As Reismann (1993) notes, there is no finite recipe to check validity in qualitative research, but persuasiveness on the part of participants can be one indicator of strong internal validity. In this study, I was impressed by the intensity of the narratives. Simply, there was a gravitas to the survivors' personal accounts that is difficult to put into words. Although the types of abuse differed, the impact and internal processing of the abuse itself had profound effects for all of the survivors with whom I spoke. As a researcher with experience in qualitative interviews, I was struck by the force of the accounts that people relayed: the litigation process had been transformative in their lives, some for the better, others perhaps for the worse. In either case, survivors relayed how litigation had opened very deep wounds. Simply, their accounts were persuasive and believable.

Another indicator of the validity came through subsequent interaction with more than half of the survivors I interviewed, due to my own activity and presence in topical events[4]. In some cases, it offered me the chance to observe some of the respondents interact or speak in public settings. In other cases, the correspondence involved e-mail updates about survivors' advocacy activities. In a few cases, people kept in contact to check in on me or the status of the research. These points of contact strengthen the validity of the narrative accounts, as my observations were consistent with my interpretations of the respondents' narrative accounts.

In addition to internal validity, external validity is also a paramount concern. In any study with a small sample size, researchers must cautiously and honestly approach issues of generalizability, and this study is no exception. I reiterate that the study was not designed to test particular theories about people who litigate over clergy sexual abuse, but instead to build knowledge about a group that has not been adequately studied in the past. The sample clearly does not represent the universe of clergy sexual abuse victims, nor does it represent the universe of clergy sexual abuse victims who litigated against the Church. Still, in a qualitative study such as this, thirty-five interviews is well within the acceptable range to explore depth, albeit while in some part sacrificing the breadth of a larger, more quantitatively oriented study (Lofland 1971). With this in mind, I cautiously posit some thoughts on the generalizability of this research.

To buttress the external validity of this methodology, I included interviews with specialists who had worked extensively with this population: attorneys, paralegals, and advocates both inside and outside the Church. Their responses drew upon a more generalized depth of knowledge of the entire group of clergy sexual abuse litigants. Whereas the survivors could speak primarily for themselves and their immediate experiences with others, attorneys and advocates were able to speak about this group as a whole. Their inclusion in this study enhances the findings from the survivors.

By design, the sample of survivors is comprised of people with several unique attributes. Participants had: 1) suffered sexual abuse at the hands of Catholic priests[5], 2) gone forward to litigate the case, and 3) volunteered for this study. The first clause presupposes that the particular universe of respondents is, by definition, a group horribly violated often in multiple ways, and usually distrustful of others. The second clause narrows the population to those who have advanced through the transformation of disputes to the final stage. But the third clause, in particular, presents a unique limitation to this data. Because respondents volunteered for the study, the sample may reflect selection bias toward those victims who also are not afraid to talk openly about their history. The poor response rate from the initial invitational letter speaks to this issue directly: there is a rather large group of survivors who either do not or cannot discuss the issue. Several legal advocates relayed stories of how many of their clients had not even told their families that they had litigated. In one law firm, this happened so often that they developed a question on their intake form about whether or not the firm could leave a message on the client's home phone. Without question, anonymity and trust issues were paramount for these survivors.

A second reason for hesitancy to participate involves the history of earlier clergy sexual abuse litigation: Countersuits were common enough to make survivors nervous about talking about anything related to the abuse. The cumulative effect of these events may have skewed the sample to include only the most outspoken—perhaps even rebellious—survivors.

Anticipating selection bias, the topic of the whole pool of survivors was brought up in the interview through the questions, "What would you want people to know about survivors who litigate that you think people do not understand?" and "What are the conceptions or misconceptions about survivors?" Many survivors noted that they were in the minority in that they were attending counseling, were able to talk about the experience, and were trying to move on after the litigation. They talked about the number of others who were still actively involved in drugs and alcohol or were silent about the abuse even to their immediate family and friends. These insights should be carefully considered when interpreting the results of this study. Perhaps the people I spoke with may have fared better than others who remain both anonymous and silent.

The location of this study is also consequential with regard to external validity. As is described in the previous chapter, Boston is an unusual place in that it is so uniquely Catholic: the Church's influence extends deep into both the public and private spheres. Because of this distinctive history, it is quite likely that victims of clergy sexual abuse in other areas of the country may have very different experiences. Although I had not initially set out to interview folks outside the area, I was able to interview several survivors who litigated outside of the Boston area. These respondents gave an incredibly important insight about the peculiarity of the Boston settlement and perceptions about victims; it was clear that some other areas of the country did not experience the same changes that Boston had, particularly in that time period. Print media coverage also reflected the changes in attitudes of the larger communities.

Conclusions

Finally, although there are caveats to the interpretations of these data, I suspect that there is much generalizability to respondents' accounts. While clearly participants have a unique story to tell, themes emerged from the data that reflect issues that are germane to the nature of the dynamic process of dispute transformation, and how experiences become defined as meriting litigation as a means of resolution. Such data can illuminate not only why these specific victims went forward with litigation, but also the thought processes that signal shifts in transforming injurious experiences into grievances, grievances into disputes, and disputes into claims in civil court.

---

[1] All interviews started by discussing the informed consent, which had been vetted thoroughly through Northeastern University's Human Subjects Board. Because of the nature of the topic, as well as the vulnerability of the population I was working with, this consent was extensive and thorough.

[2] For example, in an instance where a Church official responded somewhat poorly to victim concerns, a member of the Church actually verified the incident, as this person was present during the interaction.

[3] There are several reasons for these protections. First, I wanted to protect the survivors' identities in general. Second, I wanted to make every attempt to filter any identifying information from my field notes so that they would not be useful in any potential countersuits (See Stone 2002; Palys and Loman 2002; Palys and Loman 2000; Scarce 1994 for a discussion on the law protecting research subjects). Such countersuits by the Church had been common in prior years, and the triple blind filtration system which I employed helps to disconnect any specific comments from individual survivors. Even when survivors went public with comments, I have tried to eliminate any overlapping information from media accounts and this research so that survivors' identities are protected.

[4] First, I attended several community events that survivors attended. At these events, I was able to meet with folks with whom I had previously spoken. In every instance, I placed their anonymity paramount, as I would not initiate contact in front of other people. Instead, most of the people I recognized sought me out first, several of whom came up to give me a hug and find out about the progress of my research. I was heartened that I was treated warmly by everyone whom I interviewed. In addition to seeing survivors at community events, several other survivors kept in email contact with me as different events would come up. Two survivors e-mailed me to let me know about their own advocacy projects. The continued contact afforded me a glimpse at finding out how people were doing in their own healing journeys.

[5] It is probably important to add here that, although this study did not fact-check every piece of information given to me by the respondents, it is my belief that every person with whom I spoke who had made a claim of abuse was, in fact, being truthful to the best of their abilities. I did not doubt the veracity of the abuse claims of any of the survivors with whom I spoke.

Appendix B
Interview Protocol

First, I'd like to talk a little about your personal history. Tell me a little about your background. What was your family like? Who did you live with growing up?

Tell me about what role the Church played in your and your family's life growing up.

How did you know the priest who was the subject of your lawsuit? What was your relationship like with him before? What was his relationship with your family?

I'd like to talk to you now about what happened next. Did you talk to anyone about the abuse, and if so, who? When did you first tell someone about the abuse? Could you talk a little about who you told and what their reaction was?

When did you decide to go to law? How and why did you get involved? Did you try other alternatives prior to litigation? If so, how did they turn out? Were any alternatives closed to you that you would have liked to pursue? How have your goals changed, if at all? Did you achieve those goals? What is most important to you to achieve now? What does "justice" mean to you in this context?

Could you talk a little about how this litigation has affected you and those close to you? What do you see as consequences of the civil suit?

I understand that many victims/survivors met either through the attorneys' meetings or as part of an advocacy group. Did you take part in any of these meetings? What kinds of activities that involved meeting with other victims/survivors were you involved in? How, if at all, did these activities affect you (positively or negatively)? At any point did you feel that this connected you with a support network? How so?

Over the last two years, a great deal has happened regarding the Catholic Church in Boston. What do you think about the hundreds of victims who have come forward? When you think about it, how do you feel about the Archdiocese's responses to those victims? How do you feel about the class action suits filed against the Archdiocese?

Currently, there are statutes of limitation regarding how long a victim has to report a sex crime. Are you familiar with these laws? Given your experiences, what recommendations would you make regarding the statute of limitations for sexual abuse? Why? Could social service professionals and criminal justice professionals better respond to individuals in similar situations? If so, how? Did these laws affect you and the people closest to you (wife, children, etc.)?

Currently, priests in many states do not have to report abuse to social service agencies. Do you think this is appropriate? Why/why not? What are your feelings about these types of exceptions to the law? What do you think should be done?

How do you think the general public views survivors of clergy sexual abuse who have litigated? What do you think are the common conceptions about this group of victims? Do you believe these are accurate? Why? Specifically, what would you want people to know about you and your experience?

Now that the case is settled, tell me about your present relationship to the Church. What is your current relationship to the Catholic faith?

References

Ackerman, Robert M. 2002. "Disputing Together: Conflict Resolution and the Search for Community." *Ohio State Journal on Dispute Resolution* 18: 27-92.

Adams-Tucker, C. 1982. "Proximate Effects of Sexual Abuse in Children." *American Journal of Psychiatry* 139: 1252-1256.

Alford, Robert R. 1998. *The Craft of Inquiry: Theories, Methods, and Evidence.* New York: Oxford Press.

Angell, Marcia. 1995. *Science on Trial.* New York: W.W. Norton and Company.

Antilla, Susan. 2003. *Tales from the Boom Boom Room: The Landmark Legal Battles that Exposed Wall Street's Shocking Culture of Sexual Harassment.* New York: HarperCollins.

Associated Press. 2003. "Talks Set on Abuse by Priests as California Eases Suit Limit." *The New York Times*, January 3.

Balboni, Jennifer M. and Bishop, Donna M. 2010. "Transformative Justice: Survivor Perspectives on Clergy Sexual Abuse Litigation. *Contemporary Justice Review*, 13:133-154.

Benyei, Candice R. 1998. *Understanding Clergy Misconduct in Religious Systems: Scapegoating, Family Secrets, and the Abuse of Power.* New York: The Hayworth Pastoral Press.

Bera, Walter H. 1995. "Betrayal: Clergy Sexual Abuse and Male Survivors." In *Breach of Trust*, edited by John C. Gonsiorek, 91-111. Thousand Oaks, California: Sage Publications.

Berry, Jason. 2000. *Lead Us Not into Temptation: Catholic Priests and the Sexual Abuse of Children.* Chicago: University of Illinois Press.

Bishops' Committee of the Confraternity of Christian Doctrine (Sponsors). *The New American Bible.* Washington D.C.: Catholic Educational Guild.

Blumer, Herbert. 1969. *Symbolic Interactionism: Perspective and Method.* Los Angeles: University of California Press.

Braithwaite, John. 1998. *Crime, Shame and Reintegration.* London: Cambridge University Press.

Brajuha, Mario, and Lyle Hallowell. 1986. "Legal Intrusion and the Politics of Fieldwork: The Impact of the Brajuha Case." *Urban Life* 14: 454-478.

Briere, John N. 1992. *Child Abuse Trauma: Theory and Treatment of the Lasting Effects.* California: Sage Publications.

Briere, John, D. Evans, M. Runtz, and T. Wall. 1988. "Symptomalogy in Men Who were Molested as Children: A Comparison Study." *American Journal of Orthopsychiatry* 58: 457-461.

Brown, Jennifer G. 2004. "Symposium: The Role of Apology in Negotiation." *Marquette Law Review* 87: 665-674.

Burroughs, M. 1992. *The Road to Recovery: A Healing Journey for Survivors of Clergy Sexual Abuse*. Chatham, Massachusetts: Island Scribe.

Bruni, Frank, and Elinor Burkett. 2002. *Gospel of Shame, Children, Sexual Abuse and the Catholic Church*. New York: Perennial.

Bumiller, Kristen. 1988. *The Civil Rights Society: The Social Construction of Victims*. Baltimore: Johns Hopkins University Press.

Campbell, Donald, and Julian Stanley. 1963. *Experimental and Quasi-experimental Designs for Research*. Chicago: Rand McNally.

Catholic News Agency. 2010. "Supreme Court Allows Sex Abuse Case Against Vatican to Succeed." June 28. Accessed 6/28/2010. http://www.catholicnewsagency.com/news/supreme-court-allows-sex-abuse-case-against-vatican-to-proceed.

Clark, Donald. 1993. "Sexual Abuse in the Church: The Law Steps In." *Christian Century*, April 14.

Connors, Canice. 1994. "The Moment After Suffering: Lessons from the Pedophilia Scandal." *Commonweal*, October 21.

Cook, Judith, and Mary Margaret. 1986. "Knowledge and Women's Interests: Issues of Epistemology and Methodology in Feminist Sociological Research." *Sociological Inquiry* 56: 2-29.

Cooper-White, Pamela. 1991. "Soul Stealing: Power Relations in Pastoral Sexual Abuse." *Christian Century*, February 20.

Cornell, Bradford. 1990. "The Incentive to Sue: An Option-Pricing Approach." *The Journal of Legal Studies* 29: 73-191.

Cullen, Kevin. 2004. "Despite Settlement, Victims Struggle to Ease the Pain." *The Boston Globe,* November 15.

DeFuentes, Nanette. 1999. "Hear Our Cries: Victim-Survivors of Clergy Sexual Misconduct." In *Bless Me Father for I Have Sinned: Perspectives on Sexual Abuse Committed by Roman Catholic Priests*, edited by Thomas Plante, 135-170. Westport: Praeger.

DeYoung, Mary. 1982. *Sexual Victimization of Children*. Jefferson, North Carolina: MacFarland.

DeYoung, Mary. 1985. *Incest: An Annotated Bibliography*. Jefferson, North Carolina: MacFarland.

Dimock, Peter T. 1988. "Adult Males Sexually Abused as Children." *Journal of Interpersonal Violence* 3: 203-221.

Disch, Elizabeth, and Nancy Avery. 2001. "Sex in the Consulting Room, the Examining Room, and the Sacristy: Survivors of Sexual Abuse by Professionals." *American Journal of Orthopsychiatry* 71: 204-217.

Doe v. Creighton. 439 Mass. 281.

Doyle, Tom. 2004, November. Plenary Session. *Voice of the Faithful Annual Meeting*. Worcester, Massachusetts.

Doyle, Tom. 2003. "Roman Catholic Clericalism, Religious Duress, and Clergy Sexual Abuse." *Pastoral Psychology* 51: 181-229.

Dunn, Jennifer. 2010. *Judging Victims: Why We Stigmatize Survivors, and How They Reclaim Respect.* Boulder: Lynne Rennier Publishers.

Ellikson, Robert C. 1991. *Order Without Law: How Neighbors Settle Disputes*. Cambridge: Harvard University Press.

Epstein, Richard. 2002. "The Disclosure Dilemma: Why a Ban on Secret Settlements Does More Harm Than Good." *The Boston Globe*, November 3.

Erichson, Howard. 2003. "Beyond the Class Action: Lawyer Loyalty and Client Autonomy in Non-Class Collective Representation." University of Chicago Legal Forum: 1-45. http://papers.ssrn.com/sol3/papers.cfm?abstract _id=389161.

Farragher, Thomas. 2002. "The Cardinal Resigns." *The Boston Globe*, December 14.

Felstiner, William, Richard Able, and Austin Sarat. 1981. "The Emergence of Transformation of Disputes: Naming, Blaming and Claiming..." *Law and Society Review* 15: 631-654.

Fiftal, Emily. 1993. "Respecting Litigants' Privacy and Public Needs: Striking a Middle Ground in an Approach to Secret Settlements." *Case Western Reserve Law Review* 54: 503-572.

Finkelhor, David. 2003. "The Legacy of the Clergy Abuse Scandal." *Child Abuse and Neglect* 27: 1225-1229.

Finkelhor, David, Gerald Hotaling, I.A. Lewis, and Christine Smith. 1989. "Sexual Abuse and Its Relationship to Later Sexual Satisfaction, Marital Status, Religion and Attitudes." *Journal of Interpersonal Violence* 4: 379-399.

Fortune, Rev. Marie. 1990. *Is Nothing Sacred? When Sex Invades the Pastoral Relationship*. Thousand Oaks: Sage Publications.

Fortune, Rev. Marie. 1989. Betrayal of the Pastoral Relationship: Sexual Contact by Pastors and Pastoral Counselors. In *Psychotherapists Sexual Involvement with Clients: Intervention and Prevention*, edited by Gary Schoener. 81-91. Minneapolis: Walk-In Counseling Center.

Francis, Perry, and Nancy Turner. 1995. "Sexual Misconduct within the Church: Who are the Perpetrators and Those They Victimize?" *Counseling and Values* 39: 218-227.

Frawley-O'Dea, Mary Gail. 2005. "Experts on Sex Offenders Have News for Vatican." *National Catholic Reporter,* December 9.

Frawley-O'Dea, Mary Gail. 2004. "The History and Consequences of the Sexual-Abuse Crisis in the Catholic Church." *Studies in Gender and Sexuality* 5: 11-30.

Fromuth, Mary, and Barry Burkhart. 1987. "Childhood Sexual Victimization Among College Men: Definitional and Methodological Issues." *Violence and Victims* 2: 241-253.

Galanter, Marc. 1974. "Why the Haves Come Out Ahead: Speculations on the Limits of Legal Change." *Law and Society* 9: 95-160.

Gavrielides, Theo, and Dale Coker. 2005. "Restoring Faith: Resolving the Roman Catholic Church's Sexual Scandals through Restorative Justice." *Contemporary Justice Review* 8: 345-365.

Gaylor, Annie Laurie. 1988. *Betrayal of Trust: Clergy Sexual Abuse of Children.* Madison, Wisconsin: Freedom From Religion Foundation, Inc.

Gibson, David. 2003. *The Coming Catholic Church: How the Faithful are Shaping a New American Catholicism*. San Francisco: HarperCollins.

Gilgoff, Dan. 2010. "Catholic Church's Sexual Abuse Scandal Goes Global." *CNN online*. Accessed March 20, 2010. http://edition.cnn.com/2010 /WORLD/europe/03/19/catholic.church.abuse/index.html.

Givelber, Dan, and Anthony Robbins. 2006. "Public Health vs. Court-Sponsored Secrecy." *Law and Contemporary Problems* 169:131-140.

Goffman, Erving. 1986. *Frame Analysis. An Essay in the Organization of Experience.* Boston: Northeastern University Press.

Goffman, Erving. 1963. *Stigma: Notes on the Management of Spoiled Identity.* New York: Simon and Schuster.

Goffman, Erving. 1959. *The Presentation of Self in Everyday Life.* New York: Doubleday Books.

Goodstein, Laurie, and Michael Luo. 2010. "Pope Puts Off Punishing Abusive Priest." *The New York Times*, April 9.

Goodstein, Laurie. 2004. "Abuse Scandal is Now History, Top Bishop Says." *The New York Times*, February 28.

Goodstein, Laurie. 2002. "Victims' Group Uses Spotlight to Seek Changes in the Law." *The New York Times*, May 10.

Groome, Thomas. 2002. *What Makes Us Catholic.* San Francisco: Harper San Francisco.

Hagan, John. 1982. "Victims before the Law: A Study of Victim Involvement in the Criminal Justice Process." *The Journal of Criminal Law and Criminology* 73: 317-330.

Harr, Jonathan. 1995. *A Civil Action.* New York: Vintage Books.

Harris, Michael. 1990. *Unholy Orders: Tragedy in Mount Cashel.* New York: Viking Press.

Horst, Elizabeth. 1998. Collegeville, Minnesota: The Liturgical Press.

House of Representatives, Commonwealth of Massachusetts. 2004. House Bill 1892.

House of Representatives, Commonwealth of Massachusetts. 2004. House Bill 1893.

House of Representatives, Commonwealth of Massachusetts. 2004. House Bill 1894.

House of Representatives, Commonwealth of Massachusetts. 2004. House Bill 1895.

House of Representatives, Commonwealth of Massachusetts. 2004. House Bill 1896.

Hunter, Mic. 1990. *Abused Boys: The Neglected Victims of Sexual Abuse.* Fawcett Columbine, New York: Ballantine Books.

The Investigative Staff of *The Boston Globe.* 2002. *Betrayal: The Crisis in the Catholic Church.* Boston: Little, Brown and Company.

Isely, Peter J. 1997. "Child Sexual Abuse and the Catholic Church: An Historical and Contemporary Review." *Pastoral Counseling* 45: 277-299.

Jenkins, Philip. 1995. *Pedophiles and Priests: Anatomy of a Contemporary Crisis.* Oxford: Oxford University Press.

Jones, Ashby. 2010. "Plaintiffs Drop Sex-Abuse Suit Against Vatican." *The Wall Street Journal.* August 11. Accessed August 24, 2010. http://online.wsj.com/article/NA_WSJ_PUB:SB1000142405274870343510 4575421443951992242.html.

Kennedy, Eugene. 1993. "The See-No-Problem, Hear-No-Problem, Speak-No Problem Problem." *National Catholic Reporter*, March 19.

Kung, Hans. 2003. *The Catholic Church: A Short History.* New York: The Modern Library.

Landinsky, Jack, and Charles Susmilch. 1983. "Community Factors in the Brokerage of Consumer Product and Service Problems." Working Paper

#1983-14, Disputes Processing Research Program, University of Wisconsin, Madison.

Latif, Elizabeth. 2001. "Note: Apologetic Justice: Evaluating Apologies Tailored Toward Legal Solutions." *Boston University Law Review* 81: 289-320.

Latza Nadeau, Barbie. 2010. "The Cardinal Who Got Away." *The Daily Beast.* May 11. Accessed September 27, 2010. http://www.thedailybeast.com /blogs-and-stories/2010-05-11/the-cardinal-who-got-away.

Lee, Raymond M. 1993. *Doing Research on Sensitive Topics.* London: Sage Publications.

Levi, Deborah. 1997. "The Role of Apology in Mediation." *New York University Law Review* 72: 1165-1210.

Lew, Mike. 1990. *Victims No Longer: Men Recovering From Incest and Other Sexual Child Abuse.* New York: Harper and Row.

Libreria Editrice Vaticana. 1993. *Catechism of the Catholic Church.* San Francisco: Ignatius Press.

Lind, Edgar, and Tom Tyler. 1988. *The Social Psychology of Procedural Justice.* New York: Plenum Press.

Lofland, John. 1971. *Analyzing Social Settings.* Belmont, California: Wadsworth.

Luban, David. 1995. "Settlements and the Erosion of the Public Realm." *Georgetown Law Journal* 83: 2619-2662.

Lytton, Timothy. 2008. *Holding Bishops Accountable: How Lawsuits Helped the Catholic Church Confront Clergy Sexual Abuse.* Cambridge, Massachusetts: Harvard University Press.

MacCoun, Robert. 1988. *Alternative Adjudication: An Evaluation of the New Jersey Automobile Arbitration Program.* Santa Monica: Rand Corporation.

Makkai, Toni, and John Braithwaite. 1994. "Reintegrative Shaming and Compliance with Regulatory Standards." *Criminology* 32: 361-385.

Maris, Margo, and Kevin McDonough. 1995. "How Churches Respond to the Victims and Offenders of Clergy Sexual Abuse." In *Breach of trust*, edited by John C. Gonsiorek, 348-367. Thousand Oaks, California: Sage Publications.

Mather, Lynn, and Barbara Yngvesson. 1981. "Language, Audience, and the Transformation of Disputes." *Law and Society Review* 15: 775-821.

May, Marlynn, and Daniel Stengel. 1990. "Who Sues Their Doctors? How Patients Handle Medical Grievances." *Law and Society Review* 24: 107-120.

McCann, I. Lisa, David Sakeim, and Daniel Abrahamson. 1988. "Trauma and Victimization: A Model of Psychological Adaptation." *The Counseling Psychologist* 16: 531-594.

McDonald, Henry. 2009. "Endemic Rape and Abuse of Children in Catholic Care, Inquiry Finds." *The Guardian.* May 20. Accessed September 27, 2010. www.guardian.co.uk/world/2009/may/20/irish-catholic-schools-child-abuse-claims.

McLaughlin, Barbara R. 1994. "Devastated Spirituality: The Impact of Clergy Sexual Abuse on the Survivor's Relationship with God and the Church. *Sexual Addiction and Compulsivity* 1: 145-157.

McNamara, Eileen. 2005. "What About Girl Victims?" *The Boston Globe,* December 4.

McNamara, Eileen. 2003. "Tactics Suit the Guilty." *The Boston Globe*, April 9.

McNamara, Eileen. 2002. "A Prelate's Pretense." *The Boston Globe*, May 5.

McNulty, Craig, and Jane Wardle. 1994. "Adult Disclosure of Sexual Abuse: A Primary Cause of Psychological Distress?" *Child Abuse and Neglect* 18: 549-555.

Mendel, Matthew P. 1995. *The Male Survivor: The Impact of Sexual Abuse.* Thousand Oaks: Sage Publications.

Menkel-Meadow, Carrie. 1995. "Whose Dispute Is It Anyway? A Philosophical and Democratic Defense of Settlement (in Some Cases)." *Georgetown Law Journal* 83: 2663-2696.

Miethe, Terance. 1995. "Predicting Future Litigiousness." *Justice Quarterly* 12: 563-581.

Miller, Richard, and Austin Sarat. 1980-1981. "Grievances, Claims, and Disputes: Assessing the Adversary Culture." *Law and Society Review* 15: 525-565.

Minow, Martha. 1998. *Between Vengeance and Forgiveness.* Boston: Beacon Press.

Mishler, Elliot. 1986. *Research Interviewing: Context and Narrative.* Cambridge, Massachusetts: Harvard University Press.

Morgan, Phoebe. 1999. "Risking Relationships: Understanding the Litigation Choices of Sexually Harassed Women." *Law and Society Review* 33: 67-92.

Morris, Charles. 1997. *American Catholic: The Saints and Sinners Who Built America's Most Powerful Church.* New York: Times Books, Random House.

Mouton, Reverend Ray, Father Tom Doyle, and Father M. Peterson.1985. "The Problem of Sexual Molestation by Roman Catholic Clergy: Meeting the Problem in a Comprehensive and Responsible manner." *A Report to the United States Council of Catholic Bishops.* Washington D.C.

Muller, James, and Charles Kenney. 2004. *Keep the Faith, Change the Church.* USA: Rodale Press.

O'Brien, Victoria. 1992. *Civil Remedies for Crime Victims.* Washington D.C.: U.S. Department of Justice.

O'Connor, Thomas. 1998. *Boston Catholics: A History of the Church and Its People.* Boston: Northeastern University Press.

Olsen, P. 1990. "The Sexual Abuse of Boys: A Study of the Long-Term Psychological Effects." In *The Sexually Abused Male: Vol. 1 Prevalence, Impact and Treatment*, edited by Mic Hunter, 137-152. Lexington, Massachusetts: Lexington Books.

Owen, Richard, and Roger Boyes. 2010. "Attacks on Pope Over Child Sexual Abuse Scandal are Akin to Anti-Semitism." *The Times Online*. April 2. Accessed August 30, 2010. Accessed Month Day, Year. http://www.timesonline.co.uk/tol/comment/faith/article7086143.ece.

Palys, Ted, and John Lowman. 2002. "Anticipating Law: Research Methods, Ethics, and the Law of Privilege." *Sociological Methodology* 32: 1-17.

Palys, Ted, and John Lowman. 2000. "Ethical and Legal Strategies for Protecting Confidential Research Information." *Canadian Journal of Law and Society* 15: 39-80.

Paulson, Michael. 2002. "Church Reaction: Law's Explanation Finds Some Skeptics." *The Boston Globe*, May 21.

Pudelski, Christopher. 2004. "The Constitutional Fate of Mandated Reporting Statutes and Clergy-Communicant Privilege in a Post-Smith World." *Northwestern University Law Review* 98: 703-738.

Putnam, Robert. 2000. *Bowling Alone*. New York: Simon and Schuster.

Ranalli, Ralph. 2003. "Clergy Abuse Settlement Seen Unlikely." *The Boston Globe*, May 19.

Reissman, Catherine. 1993. *Narrative Analysis*. Newbury Park: Sage Publications.

Robinson, B.A. 2002. "Sexual Abuse by Catholic Clergy: The Canadian Situation." *Religious Tolerance.org*. March 26. Accessed August 30, 2010. www.religioustolerance.org/clergysex3.htm.

Robinson, Walter, and Stephen Kurkjian. 2002. "Archdiocese Weighs Bankruptcy Filing Facing Lawsuits: Aids Urge Chapter 11." *The Boston Globe*, December 1.

Rossetti, Stephen J. 1996. *A Tragic Grace: The Catholic Church and Child Sexual Abuse*. Collegeville, Minnesota: The Liturgical Press.

Russell, Diana E. 1986. *The Secret Trauma: Incest in the Lives of Girls and Women*. New York: Basic Books.

Sanders, Joseph. 1998. *Bendectin on Trial: A Study of Mass Tort Litigation*. Ann Arbor: The University of Michigan Press.

Santoro-Tomlin, Susan. 1991. "Stigma and Incest Survivors." *Child Abuse and Neglect* 15: 557-556.

Sauzier, M. 1989. "Disclosure of Childhood Sexual Abuse: For Better or For Worse." *Psychiatric Clinics of North America* 12: 455-469.

Scarce, Rik. 1994. "(No) Trial (But) Tribulations: When Courts and Ethnography Conflict." *Journal of Contemporary Ethnography* 23: 123-149.

Scheff, Thomas, and Suzanne Retzinger. 1991. *Emotions and Violence: Shame and Rage in Destructive Conflicts*. Originally published by Lexington. Lincoln, Nebraska: IUniversity, Inc.

Schoener, Gary R., and J. H. Milgrom. 1990. "Sexual Exploitation by Clergy and Pastoral Counselors." In *Psychotherapists Sexual Involvement with Clients: Intervention and Prevention*, edited by Gary Schoener, 225-234. Minneapolis: Walk-In Counseling Center.

Schuck, Peter. 1987. *Agent Orange on Trial: Mass Toxic Disasters in the Courts*. Cambridge: Belknap Press of Harvard University.

Second Vatican Council. 1962-1965. *The Dogmatic Constitution on the Church*. Accessed October 4, 2010. www.vatican.va/archive/hist_councils/ii _vatican_council/index.htm.

Sherman, Lawrence. 1993. "Defiance, Deterrence, and Irrelevance: A Theory of the Criminal Sanction." *Journal of Research in Crime and Delinquency* 30: 445-473.

Simon, J. Minos. 1993. *Law in the Cajun Nation*. Lafayette, Louisiana: Prescott Press.

Simpson, Victor. 2010. "Vatican Lashes Out at *The New York Times* Over Sex Abuse Coverage." *The Huffington Post*. April 1. Accessed September 27, 2010. http://www.huffingtonpost.com/2010/04/01/vatican-lashes-out-at-new_n_521544.html.

Sloan, Frank, and Chee Ruey Hsiesch. 1995. "Injury, Liability, and the Decision to File a Medical Malpractice Claim." *Law and Society Review* 29: 413-433.

Steinfels, Peter. 2003. *A People Adrift: The Crisis of the Roman Catholic Church in America.* New York: Simon and Schuster.

Stone, Geoffrey. 2002. "Discussion: Above the law—Research methods, Ethics and the Law of Privilege." *Sociological Methodology* 32: 19-27.

Strang, Heather, and Lawrence Sherman. 1997. *The Victims' Perspective.* Canberra: Australian National University Press.

Tran, Mark. 2010. "Pope Benedict Condemns 'Petty Gossip' Over Child Sexual Abuse Scandal." *The Guardian*. March 28. Accessed September 30, 2010. http://www.guardian.co.uk/world/2010/mar/28/pope-condemns-critics-catholic-sexual-abuse.

Tyler, Tom. 1990. *Why People Obey the Law*. New Haven: Yale University Press.

Ullman, Sarah, and Judith Siegel. 1993. "Victim-Offender Relationship and Sexual Assault." *Violence and Victims* 8: 121-133.

Urquiza, Anthony, and M. Capra. 1990. "The Impact of Sexual Abuse: Initial and Long Term Effects. In *The Sexually Abused Male: Vol. 1 Prevalence, Impact and Treatment*, edited by Mic Hunter, 105-136. Lexington, Massachusetts: Lexington Books.

Wagner, Wendy. 2004. "Commons Ignorance: The Failure of Environmental Law to Produce Needed Information on Health and the Environment." *Duke Law Journal* 53: 1619–1746.

Weigel, George. 2002. *The Courage to be Catholic: Crisis, Reform and the Future of the Church.* New York: Basic Books.

Weihe, Vernon, and Ann Richards. 1995. *Intimate Betrayal: Understanding and Responding to the Trauma of Acquaintance Rape*. Thousand Oaks: Sage Publications.

Weiss, Robert. 1994. *Learning from Strangers: The Art and Method of Qualitative Interview Studies*. New York: The Free Press.

Wilgoren, Jodi. 2002. "At Forum, Victims of Clergy Plead and Vent." *The New York Times,* October 24.

Winfield, Nicole. 2010a. "Vatican Says Document Does Not Prove Cover-Up." *The Boston Globe*. May 17.

Winfield, Nicole. 2010b. "Relationship Between Pope and Bishops Key in Sex Abuse Lawsuits." *The Boston Globe*, May 19.

Zezima, Katie. 2002. "Massachusetts: Criticizing Limits on Rape Charges." *The New York Times,* June 28.

Zitrin, Richard. 1999. "The Case Against Secret Settlements (Or What You Don't Know Can Hurt You)." *Journal of the Institute for the Study of Legal Ethics* 2: 115.

Index

About the Book

Why did victims of Catholic clergy sexual abuse wait so long to come forward, and what did their recourse to the courts finally achieve?

Jennifer Balboni explores the experiences of clergy sex abuse survivors who sought justice through the court system, highlighting the promise and shortfalls of civil litigation in providing justice. Balboni draws on cases across the country such as the landmark 2002 lawsuit against the Roman Catholic Church to show how legal procedures that focused on financial settlements overlooked the survivors' overarching desire to see the Church publicly acknowledge its wrongdoing. Her analysis underscores the gap between public and legal perceptions of justice and gives fresh insight into the complex ways that civil litigation can transform the lives of crime victims.

Jennifer M. Balboni is assistant professor of criminal justice at Curry College.